Trust Your Senses

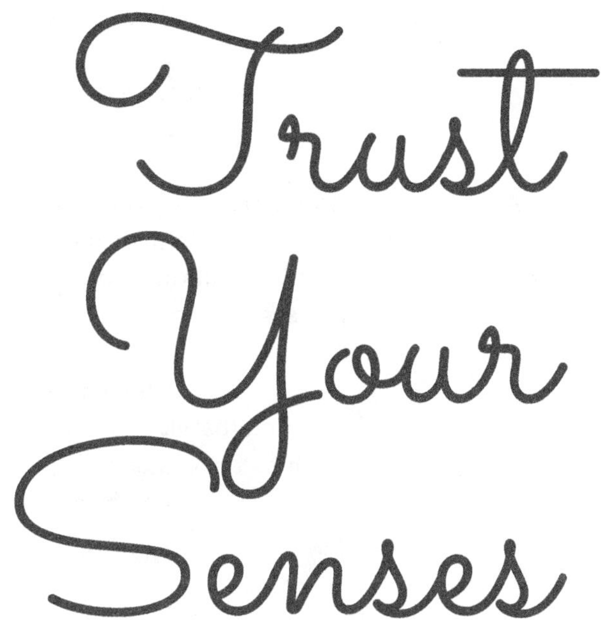

Embodied Wisdom
for the Modern Age

Deb Lange

First published 2016
Published by Lange Development Pty Ltd

Author contact: deborahlange@me.com

Cover image by Sue Stack
Internal illustrations Copyright © Sue Stack
Sue Stack, PHd, is an artist, educator and researcher interested in fostering transformation and deep connection with self, others and planet earth. www.stack.bigpondhosting.com

Typesetting by BookPOD

Disclaimer

Printed and bound in Australia by BookPOD

A Cataloguing-in-Publication entry is available from the National Library of Australia

ISBN: 978-0-9954372-0-3 eISBN: 978-0-9954372-1-0

This RELEASE AND INDEMNITY AGREEMENT (RELEASE) is voluntarily and knowingly entered into by you, hereinafter READER, and Lange Development Pty Ltd otherwise known as Deb Lange and deblange.com, its owners, employees, officers and directors, hereinafter collectively referred to as PROVIDER.

PROVIDER, Deb Lange, has professional qualifications including a Masters Degree, Bachelor Degree and Certificates in such fields as Human Resource Development, Social Ecology, Coaching, Holistic Human Development, InnerBondingTM, InterPlay, NLP, Equine Facilitated Learning and more. Coaching, Mentoring, Online Programs, documents, books, guides, audios and videos are educational in nature and the Reader takes responsibility for their own learning. As a reader of this material you, the reader accept full responsibility for your own actions and will consult with a professional about your own circumstances before following anything in this book. Results are not guaranteed. The author and publisher make no warranties of any kind, express or implied, with regard to the content or accuracy.

Coaching, facilitation and educational resources are not to be construed or understood to fall into the category of professional psychological counselling or psychiatric services. PROVIDER does not purport to be a credentialed psychological therapist, counsellor, or qualified medical or psychiatric therapist or interventionist.

Readers and participants release Deborah Lange and Lange Development Pty Ltd from any liability.

STATEMENT FROM READER AND WEBSITE VISITOR: By registering for the website and purchasing or reading any free materials I give notice that I understand the declaration that is published above, and I willingly proceed to this site and take responsibility in full for any actions I proceed to take as a result of reading this educational material.

Heart
open
allow for
playfulness

Contents

The Guest House
A poem by Rumi [1]

This being human is a guest house.
Every morning a new arrival.

A joy, a depression, a meanness,
some momentary awareness comes
as an unexpected visitor.

Welcome and entertain them all!
Even if they're a crowd of sorrows,
who violently sweep your house
empty of its furniture, still,
treat each guest honourably.
He may be clearing you out
for some new delight.

The dark thought, the shame, the malice,
meet them at the door laughing
and invite them in.
Be grateful for whoever comes,
because each has been sent
as a guide from beyond.

1 https://theheartofawakening.wordpress.com/2013/07/10/poem-of-the-week-the-guest-house-by-rumi/

Sue

Preface

The purpose of a book is to serve as an
axe for the frozen sea within us.
—Franz Kafka[2]

As a child, I was intrigued by the difference between happy times and upset times between my family members. These experiences raised many childhood questions: What caused the upset? How could I mediate peace? How do relationships shift so quickly from contentment to conflict? What unknown problems did my father have that he was peaceful and loving at times and worried and anxious the next?

My childhood became my first playground for discovering human, physical and energetic dynamics. My family experiences sparked my passion for becoming a social scientist. I pursued qualifications to be a successful educator, facilitator and mentor in the workplace and for people's personal lives.

The workplace became my new playground for understanding people, and discovering that people cut themselves in two: taking on a professional persona at work and becoming personal at home. Cutting ourselves in two and thinking we can be logical in one place and emotional in another doesn't work very well.

I worked with people who had problems at work—and those same problems were often mirrored at home. For example, a boss who micro-managed and over-controlled team members at work was a controlling father or husband at home. On the other hand, some managers I worked with who were perfectionists and made overwhelming demands on their teams were still managing the long-term consequences of never being good enough for a parent's approval and love. Some people were triggered by certain behaviours and others were not.

I discovered when I helped people bring a behaviour that had adverse consequences to light there was a release of that behaviour, and new behaviours that created more ease for self

2 http://www.kafka-online.info/franz-kafka-quotes.htm

and others could become new habits. When there was a change in behaviour in one place, whether that be at work or at home, the positive change rippled out successfully with other people in both their personal and professional realms. Gaining the ability to identify patterns of behaviour in our lives, creates a significant impact in overturning many obstacles.

My work with clients gave me an opportunity to explore how to re-imagine the kind of life I wish to live where I can feel my sense of aliveness and become conscious of patterns of behaviour. A life, where I can appreciate others and this wonderful place we call home, in our natural world, and all the grace, beauty and compassion that is within every moment.

My passion for understanding life is a source of boundless energy for learning. Each choice I have made, whether wise or not so wise has led me to look further, both on the outside and the inside, to find out how to make choices that lead to more fulfilment and meaning.

My quest has taken me to many places. I have had my body painted by the Himba women in Namibia, gone hunting with the bushmen in Botswana, lived in an inn in the mountains in France, been a roadie for an Irish harpist in Germany and learnt how to partner with horses to be present to our sense of being in nature. These are only a few snippets of my rich and diverse journey.

Going outside our 'normal' life has enriched my discovery of sensing, playing, synthesising, and understanding what I do or don't do, which create harmony within me and my life. In essence, I continuously learn what works and what doesn't, which helps me gain the wisdom to live my life well.

This book is about what I have learnt and is intended to guide others through the process of discovering your body's language. I have come to the conclusion, that we have a natural intelligence within our instincts, sensing and intuitive capacities that we often disregard. This is often to our detriment.

We have been focusing on the intelligence of our brain since Descartes declared the mind was disconnected from the body. While we keep on believing rational logic is our 'God', we keep thinking about things with our mind alone and become overwhelmed with the complex information we deal with on a daily basis.

The development of our logic has resulted in significant industrial and technological advances; unfortunately, it neither reduces our anxiety nor addresses our inner voices, which are often at odds with one another. In times of complexity and uncertainty, are our senses and intuition are stronger than reason?

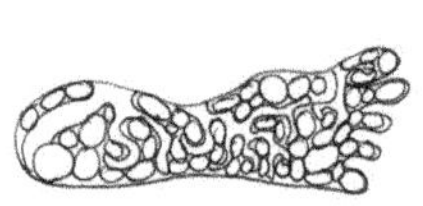

Preface

"When faced with a difficult question, we often answer an easier one instead, usually without noticing the substitution."[3]
—Daniel Kahneman

Using reason to solve our challenges has become so habitual that we avoid staying with uncertainty, feeling, sensing and intuiting patterns to lead to a different way to make our choices. Every time we discount our own or another person's feelings, we deny our humanity, which leads to confusion, stress, conflict, an overwhelming work environment and even corruption. There is now an all-time high of illnesses such as depression, stress and obesity. Could the plethora of modern-day malaise, anxiety and conflict be a result of disconnection from our body, our senses and our energy?

Rational thinking at the time of the Industrial Revolution created workplaces where humans were expected to work like machines. Unfortunately, we still live this legacy. Even when we talk about more human work practices today, unless we reveal the beliefs and values in our mindsets; our choices, work practices and culture will still reflect the image of being human as a machine that can be controlled. Control and intimidation lead to cultures and relationships based in fear. Bullying and intimidation arise from these practices. These challenges will not be solved by more control and compliance, but by changing the principles of how we live and work together based on mutual respect, trust, freedom, autonomy and cooperation. We need to grow out of them and replace our machine, control orientated beliefs and actions with those that allow us to be fully human.

We treat our body as if it is a drudge. It is never good enough. It is either too fat, to thin, too slow, gets too tired, needs feeding and exercising. We act as if we are in control of our body as if it is not a part of us. When we are living in our heads, outside our visceral experience, we disconnect from what creates our wellbeing. We misconstrue needing water for hunger. We don't know the feeling of being 'full', so we keep on eating when our body does not need more food. We misconstrue our unhappiness as something that someone else created, so we leave relationships, endlessly searching for the right one that will fulfil us. We don't sense that we need to cry to release stress so we control our tears, or we control our anger and become tight lipped and fixed in our points of view.

---

3 Daniel Kahneman, "Thinking Fast and Thinking Slow", Farrax Strous Griroux, New York, 2011 http://thebookwire.com/2015/05/22/thinking-fast-and-slow-quotes/

We have forgotten our body knows. Our body is intelligent. We have natural instincts and an inner body language that is sending us messages to bring ourselves into a state of wellness. We have forgotten how to listen. We listen to the words in our head. We listen to other people's words. When we think too much, we override our body's intelligence.

It is time to remember to connect with our heart, our 'gut', our energy, our conscience, and to sense our whole selves and the richness of the gift of our senses.

We act as if we are dismembered.

Nearly 80 years ago, Waldorf Steiner[4] developed his educational models around a belief that we have 12 senses. If our sense perceptions are half of how we make sense of the world, when we focus on thinking, and not sensing, in reductionist ways, we cut ourselves off from rich information. When we are too pre-occupied with the brain, we limit the development of our other senses.

In *The Biology of Belief*, Bruce Lipton[5] explains how our beliefs reside in our body and impact how we choose to be in this world. Language, for example, impacts our world. Words fill our life.

But language is physical. Let me say that again. Language arose from our physical and imaginary experiences.

4 http://www.waldorfhomeschoolers.com/twelve-senses
5 https://www.brucelipton.com/books/biology-of-belief

"It is beyond a doubt that all or knowledge begins with experience."
— Immanual Kant

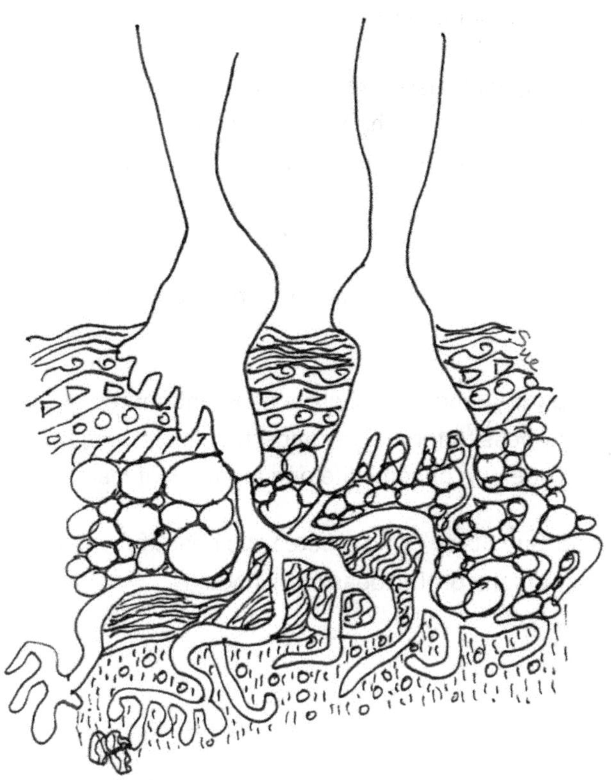

with our feet firmly on the ground

When we say words that are descriptive, they evoke emotion and connection. The more we use abstract language that does not connect us to our physical and imaginal experience the more we become dis-connected from our humanity. The more we can make choices that may be unethical, or uncaring for others. Abstractions create a void between us as we struggle to make the words relate to our experience. Emotive, imaginal, descriptive and body language creates a visceral response that helps us make meaning to connect with others.

It was my experiences in life that led me to get a sense of an inner body language and our language in our movement. I shared this understanding to my many treasured clients, and they have arrived at the same conclusion as mine. Through my guidebook, eCourse, mentoring, coaching and speaking engagements, I am facilitating many others to awaken their senses and live more richly.

As technological advances present us with ethical dilemmas, it is critical that we connect to our multiple intelligences in which our conscience is held. We need to make choices from the perspective of what enables life to thrive and co-exist.

While indigenous peoples like the Polynesian Wayfinders[6] developed 'seeing', 'sensing' and 'intuiting', we focused on rational things. Our innate sense-making capacities have been latent, waiting in the wings for us to turn and listen

I feel our senses are calling us to listen, to return to our bodies and live in an embodied state of being while we are alive on this earth. When we come home to our body and ourselves, we are richly rewarded. It is a way of feeling our sense of aliveness.

It is time.

I thank all the people who have trusted me to be their guide as we have travelled together on our journey.

My children, who are both young adults, are a constant source of insight. I thank them for their honesty and willingness to forgive my imperfections as a mother. I am proud that they, too, have taken up the quest to become lifelong pioneers of learning.

I have deep respect for Sue Stack[7], who created the beautiful painting for the cover and the drawings that represent many of the ideas in this book.

"And those who were seen dancing
were thought to be insane by those
who could not hear the music."
- Friedrich Nietzsche

6 http://www.amazon.com/Wayfinders-Ancient-Wisdom-Matters-Lecture/dp/0887847668
7 http://www.stack.bigpondhosting.com/

Navigating this book

This book has three rites of passage for your journey.

The first rite of passage—the opening

Discovering your triggers

The first rite of passage for me was uncovering one of my own significant blind spots, which led me to take this journey. In this passage, I invite you to muse on what triggers you in ways that you don't like. When do you say:

"Why do I do that?"

"Oh no, I just did that 'thing' again."

"Why does that person always press my buttons?"

If we are curious enough, these are like doors that can open within us, revealing the truth about a long-forgotten event. When we reveal the source of the trigger, we can finally resolve it and release ourselves from being stuck in the same defensive cycle.

These are the openings to release the tension that we have been hanging onto for many years. These are the openings to our freedom.

When we open that door, we can uncover something that we are doing that is not in alignment with who we are, what we believe in, and what we say or do. We can peel away a layer of protection that we may not need as an adult and finally become our truth.

Our instincts, senses and intuition are guides to help us uncover the opening. I share my story and the stories of others who also took this journey, the challenges they faced and what new tools they used to overcome those challenges.

The second rite of passage—instincts, noticing and sensing in daily life

New ways to make sense of an inner body language

In the second rite of passage, I share another story of unintended adversity that will resonate with many readers. I unravel the ways we misinterpret the messages from our body and how that leads to unfortunate and unintended consequences. When we are navigating this rite of passage, we begin listening to new guides to read the messages from an inner body language. These new guides help us navigate complexity and uncertainty with grace and ease.

The third rite of passage: new navigation guide

A series of practice guides

The third rite of passage is to practise learning new ways of seeing and experiencing our world every day. This section of the book can be used like a journal. There is an invitation to use these guides to re-discover your senses, and interpret the messages from your instincts, senses and images. There is a space for you to jot down notes, doodles, drawings and musings.

This is not a book of theory. It is a book of rites of passage through practice and an invitation for you to:

And when you do accept the invitation, please share what you are discovering with your friends, colleagues and online friends. Let's create a new 'body' of sensory knowledge: the practice of reconnecting and identifying patterns, success and obstacles to help grow our capacity to be more human.

COURAGE
COURAGE
Courage
Sue

The First Rite of Passage—the Opening

The planet does not need more 'successful' people.
But it does desperately need more peacemakers,
healers, restorers and lovers of every kind. It needs
people who live well in their places. It needs
people of moral courage willing to join the fight
to make the world habitable, just and humane.
—David Orr

RE-DEFINING SUCCESS

At the beginning my first rite of passage

A long time ago, I gained my first management consultancy contract for my solo entrepreneurial business.

I was excited. I had my freedom. I was doing what I loved.

I was proud to be contributing to workplaces where people were valued, and the organisation was thriving, ethical, creative and humane. Before I knew it, I was getting assignments nationally and internationally and being asked to open conferences and be a keynote speaker. I was doing innovative, ground-breaking work and getting paid well. Everything was great.

I was successful!

My husband's career also began to escalate successfully. He became CEO of a government organisation. His work was demanding and time-consuming.

We had a beautiful house; the kids were doing well in their private schools and then...

The cracks started to appear.

My husband and I worked well together. Both of us were happy with each other, but we were like ships passing in the night.

We had 21 happy years, but we became disconnected from one another. I said at the time, "I love you, but I don't love you." I now know that was naive. I did not know how to resolve what I was feeling. At times, this was an inner tension, at other times a blandness.

We had an amicable divorce and I took time off to recuperate and take stock. I had success with work *and* success in my relationship until the things that had never been reconciled in my life began to surface. In Jungian terms, it is called our shadow. Anything from our past that was never resolved screams out to be resolved. I could not feel and sense the love and loyalty that was present in the relationship. I was, like so many of us today, experiencing a disconnection between thought and body.

Projection

While being busy results in feelings of alienation, the source of the disconnection between what I was thinking and what I was feeling had occurred a long time ago. I was projecting unresolved issues into my present relationship. This is a common mistake. New events trigger old memories, both the good ones and the ones that we have locked away. Learning to discern the difference between what is happening right now and what is triggering habitual behaviour from a past event is critical for our success. Projection of issues onto people and events in our life today when it has nothing to do with them leads to great adversity and misunderstanding.

It was this discomfort that resulted in my understanding that I was protecting myself from feeling pain—the pain and heartache of feeling disconnected as a child when my parents had many troubles. Although I had intellectually resolved those early events, they still physically, emotionally and energetically lay under the surface. The shield I put around me distanced me from feeling and releasing the unresolved pain.

This was the way we were taught. We were told to put events behind us, not to feel pain, have a stiff upper lip and not to cry. The strategies of not experiencing emotional, psychological and physical pain may appear to resolve a situation at the time, but they perpetuate a disconnection between what we think and what we feel.

The best way to get rid of the pain is to
feel the pain. And when you feel the pain
and go beyond it, you'll see there is very
intense love wanting to awaken itself.
–Deepak Chopra

All of us experience trauma at some stage of our lives. It does not have to be major abuse. It can be the trauma of working hard to be the captain of a sports team and being overlooked, the trauma from a vindictive teacher who takes a dislike to us and leaves us feeling 'picked on', downtrodden and overlooked. It can be wanting a father or mother's approval and never seeming to be good enough. When we were young there were a zillion small ways we unintentionally made our life events tell us that we are not good enough, or loving enough, or worthy enough. Until we find out what these are, they can be the hidden force behind behaviours that limit our success as adults.

An executive I worked with revealed he was in constant competition with his team as he was still fighting his four siblings for his father's approval. Then there's the manager constantly overwhelmed by demanding perfection of herself at work who finally realised she had begun that pattern as a child to seek her father's love.

We can be highly successful in areas of our life using the strategies for success we learnt. However, all of us also had life events where we protected ourselves, did the best we could within the limitations of our abilities at the time, and these have led to us carrying unresolved issues.

We were not taught how to uncover hidden behaviours that limit our success. We were not taught how to release energy from unresolved conflicts at the time of those events. These unresolved issues do not go away. They stay stuck in our bodies and minds until we release ourselves from their limitations. If we don't, we limit our success by becoming stuck in defensive routines or being okay with the status quo. We can still be successful but we will always have an Achilles heel, which limits the freedom we can have in our lives, to be our full selves and create the kind of success we want.

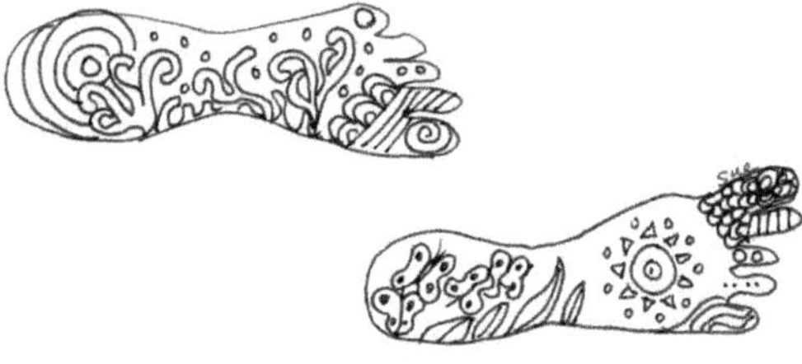

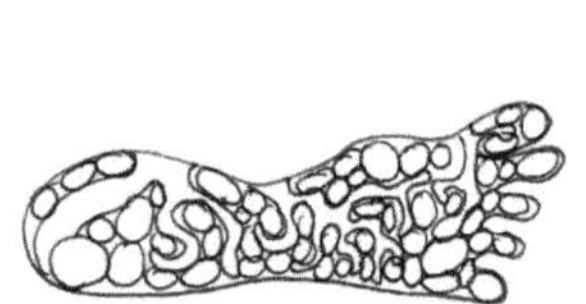

Avoidance

We avoid acknowledging our disconnection in many ways. We cover up, we become great at telling white lies to ourselves and to others or pretending we are somebody else.

A common way to avoid our disconnection is being busy and focusing on external success. Like most of us, I bought the myth that success meant working and studying hard to have it all at the same time: well-paid work; respect and fulfilment; a happy family; active participation in society and the community; physical health; perhaps being an artist, musician or gardener.

I am not alone.

Focusing on external success while overriding our inner emotional needs eventually breaks down. It is like having a weak link in a bridge or a weak container of bricks in a wall or foundation.

We want success, but at what cost?

The pretence, cover-up and avoidance of not being in our body, sensing and releasing stress, catches up with most of us. As soon as we realise that and start to get in touch with our emotions, as well as learn to hear what they are saying to us, we are released from the hold the stress has on us. Practising this as a ritual, just like brushing our teeth daily, gives us amazing internal freedom.

Do we need to rethink what success means?

Some people are gradually tearing apart the myth of perfectionism and having everything all at once. It is now a growing trend to plan a 'career pause' for a family. The youngest generations of women in the workforce—the millennials, aged 18 to early 30s—are defining career success differently and less linearly than previous generations of women. It is with much delight that I hear about families choosing to redefine success today.

My second rite of passage

My attempts to redefine success sent me on another journey. Now single, running my own business, caring for children between two homes and caring for my own home, I confronted the behaviours that limited me.

Time

Most of us say we are so busy that we do not have time to figure out why we were triggered by that team member, or by speaking in front of a group, or why we always seem to experience conflict with a particular type of person. It takes time and a conscious commitment to unravel what we are doing that is creating our success, as well as what we are doing, thinking and imagining that limits our success. We are often more stressed than we realise and we keep on going until we break down.

Have you experienced a realisation that you are extremely stressed, but, it was only when you stopped, after a period of being particularly busy? I wanted to avoid that happening to me again. I recognised that I needed more time to chill out than I had thought, and I was not going to let work and wanting to be successful in business take me away from the things that mattered to me.

That is, until another pull away from how to create success in my terms caused a downturn in my life.

Another relationship

This time, I was determined to 'make sure' the relationship was successful and I would continue to properly care for adolescent children, parents, friendships, my soul connection, my creativity and my health. It did not turn out the way I had planned. While still wanting to be successful at work, I found the second relationship demanding, demoralising and unsupportive. I could not succeed in my work while being so drained from endlessly giving without receiving any sustenance from the relationship.

Success in different disguises

Success for me at this time meant letting go of my second relationship. I let go after finally accepting the behaviour I was experiencing was not love, and it was eroding my self-worth. I had to accept I could not change this person's behaviour no matter how compassionate and understanding I became. When a person does not take responsibility for the consequences of their actions, there is nothing else to do but leave the unhealthy situation. With the erosion of my self-belief and freedom to make choices that aligned with my truth, I found it extremely challenging to be successful in my personal and work life. Fortunately, I had the strength and conviction to know that the relationship was not healthy, and that I needed it to end to create a successful life.

Success of another kind

With aging parents who needed care, I made a choice that seemed the obvious one for me, to take the time to honour my parents' wishes to age and die at home. I retired early while I self-funded a sabbatical to care for my parents.

Success at this stage of my life was getting to know my mother all over again as she aged, softening into a whole new relationship with her, which resolved any historical conflicts and misunderstandings. Her greatest wish was to die at home, with her loved ones and the familiarity of place supporting her pass over with love, dignity and respect. I was successful in her dying well. There were many treasured experiences that I would have denied myself if I had prioritised being successful in business over helping my parents die well.

The lessons I learnt about success

Between stimulus and response, there
is space. In that space is our power to
choose our response. In our response
lies our growth and our freedom.
–Viktor E. Frankl

Success is about making powerful choices in the pause between a stimulus and our response. As humans, we are blessed with the power to choose. We can make choices that are right for us but bad for others and the environment. We can also make choices that are good for both ourselves and others and our environment.

When the pause is too long and we stay with logic, rationalising why certain things are the way they are, whilst ignoring emotional and intuitive information, we limit our choices and get stuck. I learnt the discomfort of believing my logic that I could do something to "make" a relationship better, whilst ignoring my exhausted and demeaned emotional self, saying this relationship is eroding my self-worth.

When the pause is too short and we use logic alone for our choices, we also limit ourselves. We may lack compassion for ourselves, perhaps giving up our needs for others, or we may blindly be selfish and create our success at the expense of others. I do not define either of these ways as success.

One of the most important skills we can learn is self-reflection and attention to logic, emotions, physicality, story, movement and images. William Glasser, in his book *Choice Theory: A New Psychology of Personal Freedom*[8], supports one of the practices I developed, where I sense I have the power to make a choice at any moment and give up the limiting practice of blaming what has happened in the past for taking away my power to choose. At any point in time, I can choose what contributes to my well-being.

In every society, there is a common practice of staying in unhappy situations and blaming some event, person or ourselves for what we have and don't have. We have forgotten that we have the power to choose every moment of the day. Many of our choices are more about controlling another person in an effort to get them to change rather than focusing on what we have: our power to change.

We can be an authority over ourselves and our situation without needing to force others to change. We can change what is within our power to change, which is often more than what most people realise.

We can choose to change jobs if our relationship with a boss is toxic, to deepen a relationship with our spouse if we are disconnecting and to change careers if unfulfilled. We do not have to stay stuck. I am, of course, talking to the privileged people, like me, who live in developed countries and have access to education, health, safety and security.

The deep practices I developed enabled me to access information from my instincts, my senses and my intuitive abilities. These sources of information we have neglected and ignored to develop while we pursued rational thinking.

There is a story told of Christopher Columbus sailing towards the shores of America and the American Indian people not being able to see the ship on the horizon. The ship could not be seen as it had never been experienced. The story goes on to say a Shaman pointed out the ripples on the water to his companions, so the ship gradually came into view.

8 William Glasser, *Choice Theory, A New Psychology of Personal Freedom*, 1999

Similarly, we have not been able to see our instincts, our senses and our intuitive knowing while we are focusing on seeing what is rational and objective.

When we are open to multiple ways of knowing, sensing and being, we too can discover new insights that were out of our view. These new ideas expand our ways of sensing and knowing so we can make more powerful choices for our lives.

It is these sensory and intuitive skills that I have now accessed, which enabled me to co-create my world with a new definition of success. Living in connection with our senses is...

"a way of thinking enacted as much by the body as by the mind, informed by the humid air and the soil and the quality of our breathing, by the intensity of our contact with the other bodies that surround."
– David Abram[9]

It is with this kind of presence and self-reflection that we reveal our blindness of what we are doing to sabotage ourselves and what we are doing that is creating our success. In a candid and reciprocal conversation with those we trust, we can further learn the art of uncovering our blindness and shift our sense of being in ways that we have not imagined. A conversation, not only in words, but also in movement.

Throughout my mid-life journey, I learnt to deepen my practice of self-reflection,

9 David Abram, *Becoming Animal: An Earthly Cosmology*

learning the art of interpreting messages from my emotions, from sensing my energy and the physicality of my movement to the environment, people and places. I learnt to reconnect with ancient wisdom stored in my body, in much the same way as the Polynesians, or the Wayfinders, who use their sophisticated sensory and intuitive abilities to navigate the sea without instruments.

The Polynesians have a practice of grounding themselves to the centre of their being through their navel and sensing the wind, water, stars and nature to intuit their path safely through treacherous waters and live their lives.

Despite all of our scientific knowledge and technical expertise, accumulated over centuries of systematic and disciplined effort, we... overlooked until the past decade or so something like 95% of the physical content of the universe—its so-called dark matter and energy.
– Edward Kelly and David E. Presti

We are only just beginning to get skilled in reconnecting, seeing and accepting the intelligence of our senses, intuition and emotions, which are more than what our logical brain can give. It is these skills that shine the light on the 'control virus' that inhabits us in more ways than we may imagine whenever we wonder how to understand the complex situations in our lives. It is these skills that have given me the freedom to sense a grounding, in my being that allows me to intuit choices for my life.

Imagine for a moment that you are watching a movie. The movie tells a story based on beliefs about having to be in control, to dominate our world and use reason for choice. In this movie we act as if we can control our world and gain our security from owning and controlling 'things' and having power over others.

Are we controlling what needs freedom? And we wonder why, people are escaping our organizations, why people have conflict in controlling relationships!

Now watch the movie from a different lens.

The second picture sees humans inter-connected with each other and with our natural environment. People are free to adapt, create, be spontaneous and respect the interdependence we have with each other and our environment. In this situation, our security comes from a grounding within our being. Through this lens, we develop trust in ourselves and others, which invokes our cooperation with people and our environment for mutual benefit.

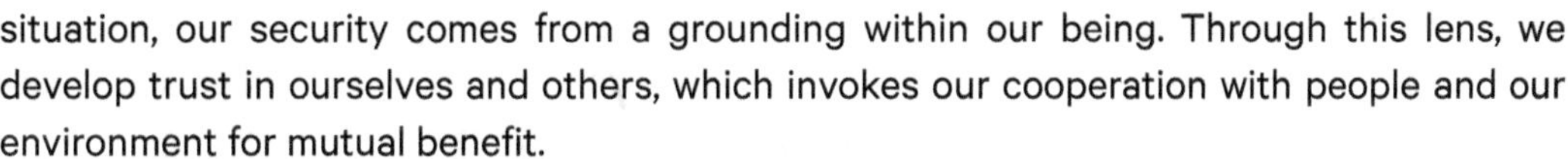

People are attracted to us when we act from our authentic self and they have the freedom to be with us. We are in transition from a world of control and compliance to a world of freedom and autonomy.

In the transition, it is the development of a deeper sense of trust within ourselves and others which will carry us on the journey.

Just as the Wayfinders learnt intuitive knowing, so can we. When we restore the connection between our thinking, sensing and intuiting, we have the capacity to redefine success and recreate our lives in ways that are beyond our current imagination.

The gap between thinking and sensing is a disconnection that we have used to protect ourselves psychologically, emotionally and energetically. When under threat, both humans and animals disconnect thought from body to protect themselves from the sensation of pain. In animals, scientists believe the disconnected state may be like creating amnesia, before being eaten by a predator.

In Western society, there is much advice to overcome the instincts of what people call our 'reptilian brain', which generates fear in response to perceived threats. We may not have woolly mammoths at every street corner, but we have predators of a different kind. Our predators today are more to do with being controlled by others. We have predators who prey on the kindness and generosity of others, and predators who inhabit the 'control virus' and bully, coerce and intimidate others.

These attacks are more often psychological, financial and emotional than physical. Although physical violence is still prevalent today, it is necessary today to understand that fear arises when we need to create safety. We need a different kind of protection than nomads or cave dwellers, but we still need to create psychological, emotional, financial and physical safety in both the workplace and at home.

We can fall into sabotaging our success through a lack of sensing controlling, predatory behaviour. We may fall into traps of being with people who manipulate a situation for their benefit to our detriment. Learning how to understand the messages from our senses and emotions from a young age enhances our opportunity to avoid being controlled and create freedom and inter-dependence to live in cooperation with others over our lifetime.

Disconnecting forces

Protection

As children, we learnt to protect ourselves from psychological and emotional harm, but many of us were not taught how to release the tension when the event is over. This unresolved tension from defending ourselves can manifest as control over others, including bullying, meanness and self-sabotage. Bullying is often a defence mechanism for unresolved early-life events, projected onto the people around us today. The better we are at sensing that we are being manipulated or bullied, the better we can be at creating boundaries of respect for ourselves and not tolerate bullying behaviour. When we disconnect from our senses, we are more likely to allow negative behaviour from another to affect us over an extended period.

Rational thinking

The disconnection between thought and our senses arises from other elements of modern-day life as well, not only traumatic events. Our obsession with rational thinking is at the expense of sensing, feeling and intuiting information from within ourselves.

Technology

There are a plethora of modern-day technologies constantly pulling us out of our bodies and away from the visceral experience of being alive and human. Technology is not going away, but, like anything, when we lose sight of using it as a tool and it becomes a way of life, it can have unintended adverse consequences.

Dependence

One additional idea that disconnects us from our body intelligence is an over-reliance on seeking answers outside ourselves from experts. In this book, it is my intention to share ways you can learn to seek out information from others, synthesise this with your own experience and make sense of what is true for you. I do not tell you your answers, I guide you to discover them for yourself.

These four elements disconnect us from our humanity, wholeness and ultimately success:

1. Psychological and physical disassociation from trauma
2. Revering rational thinking at the expense of emotional and intuitive ways of thinking
3. Using technology excessively
4. Over-reliance on outside experts for our answers.

BELLA'S JOURNEY TO OPENING

This journey to intuit and sense my truth was incremental but also a looping back and forth deepening new skills and strategies at every turn. Each new lesson took me into a new place to discover another realm of possibility.

I share a story of my path to freedom and to developing highly intuitive capabilities. I applied what I learnt with different groups of people who came to me saying they were successful in one area of their life but not in another. Usually, their success was in a technical competence but not in personal relationships or their relationship with themselves.

My guidance has worked for both men and women from different age groups, cultures and from senior executives to millennials. These guides are not necessarily the whole truth. I invite people to sense their truth and trust themselves to make sense of their life based on their own intuitive connection.

I share here a story of how Bella, a young woman who came to me for mentorship, walked through the stages of her journey to reach new success in her life and work.

Phase 1: Recognition

Bella contacted me feeling stressed after a relationship breakdown and with challenges working for a boss that she found highly controlling and demanding. Her realisation that she could live her life differently was her first step.

In our work together, Bella not only discovered that she was a perfectionist, she also uncovered the underlying reasons why she had to do things differently from how she was doing them now. She was constantly anxious and doubted her ability to create success in her life.

Phase 2: The choice

Bella paused, breathed and made the choice to self-reflect. I invited her to reflect not only on the words in her head but also how she felt and how her body was responding to what she was thinking and saying. I invited her to switch being standing and walking to sense her energy and her physical being as well as be still and reflect on the stories she shared. There was a noticeable shift in our first session. Introducing awareness of how her body moved, how she breathed and the interaction between body and words had a settling affect. She began to breathe more deeply. We talked about what she could do to care for herself.

She immediately began seeking new friendships rather than staying isolated and ashamed after her relationship breakdown. Renewed success in her personal life was beginning.

As soon as we choose to pause and deeply consider what is happening rather than continue to react to events, we are on the way to becoming more successful. Once we start, we are twice as likely to respond in ways that enhance our best interests. But, it was not only the verbal conversation that was a catalyst, it was the noticing and sensing her body awareness and movement.

Phase 3: Exformation[10]

At the beginning of an unknown journey, we are often overwhelmed with information and emotional tension. We tend to focus on informing ourselves and pay little attention to 'exforming' or emptying what we know to give space to learn something new.

When Bella began working with me she was very uptight. I guided her to do a body scan. Running her awareness over her body.

I asked, "What are you feeling?"

Bella, said, "I am too scared to cry. If I cry I will never stop and my sadness will overwhelm me."

10 The term Exformation, comes from "www.InterPlay.org" . The opposite of inform.

I talked to Bella about being safe to feel her feelings and if her body needed to cry, to give herself permission to stop controlling her body and preventing her tears. I created a safe space for her to touch her emotions and give herself permission to open the floodgates. I invited her to move, to walk, to sit, to sense her body as she moved. She moved, she sensed, she sat, she curled inwards softly and she cried, and cried and sobbed. I offered her gentle witnessing, not speaking, but being with her, affirming for her it was OK to cry. I would not humiliate, demean or rescue. I would be a companion at her side.

She stopped.

I asked, 'How are you feeling now?"

Bella, responded with joy and surprise. "I feel light and relief in my body. I feel amazed that I held on for so long when it felt so good to cry. And I stopped? I am not the snivelling mess that I thought I would be for hours, days, perhaps weeks."

Who is telling you what to do? Where do those voices in your head come from?

I taught Bella how to 'exform' emotion and energy that had been pent up and was blocking her feeling of happiness. She 'exformed' her thoughts and tension in her body through journaling and released emotions by giving herself permission to move her body and sense what she was feeling and imagining, feel her feelings no matter what they are.

Exformation increased Bella's ability to create what ease felt like in her life, many more times more than if she stayed tight with tension, blocking her ability to sense what her body needed. This was the beginning of leaning in to her body to access a new inner body language through our physicality and movement.

Phase 4: Noticing

When we pause and reflect on whether our actions align with what we say, we can reveal our truth or our blind spots. Bella became aware of her childhood belief that the only way to receive love from her parents was to become perfect. She may have understood rationally that perfection is unattainable, and even that her parents loved her anyway, but the strength of her belief was stronger than her rational mind.

Her addiction to strive for success and to never feel good enough formed when she was a child. She would work 80-hour weeks, which weakened her health. She found it difficult to say no to her boss when he requested more work. She was compelled to be the perfect partner, expecting nothing, while having to give the best of herself. Something had to give, and Bella had a relationship breakdown.

When Bella revealed her blind spots and her false beliefs, she learnt to say no to unreasonable requests that would cost her too much in time, energy and credibility. She began to create new boundaries of respect. Her behaviour influenced her boss. He began to support her rather than drive her hard.

Phase 5: Sensing

I invited Bella to play a game of sensing her energy when she woke in the morning and follow it during the day. I suggested she give herself the freedom in her lunch hour to let her body do the walking and see what she was attracted to and what she moved away from. A game to begin to notice her body and what it was sensing without controlling or telling herself what she wanted.

As she played this game, she found she was attracted to music. She took up learning to play drums. She had never thought she was interested in learning to drum, but, by giving her body the freedom to go where it felt energised, she began to discover new insights about herself.

She was now learning to sense the difference between the energy of perfection and striving, and the energy of flow and success with ease and grace. She learnt how to adapt to situations and became more resilient rather than needing the perfect answer to everything. Her definition of success was growing incrementally through her increased sensing abilities and resilience.

Phase 6: Voicing

Bella learnt to sense when she was controlling her behaviour and tolerating things in life that she could not speak up about. Previously, she could never say no to family members' requests and gave her time and money to others, leaving little or no time or resources for

herself. She felt exhausted and exploited but could not stop this debilitating behaviour. When she was controlling her feelings, she could not speak her truth as the energy of control would suddenly be released in an aggressive voice making the other person wrong.

As she learnt to sense her feelings and be with them she spoke about what was important for her before taking actions that were not self caring. She learnt a new resilience. She did not feel exhausted and angry at others for “taking from her”, as she learnt to create new boundaries of respect for herself. This gave Bella a new sense of freedom to speak her truth. She was now able to say what she felt to family members who relied on her for support. Now, with the ability to voice her truth, she increased her success in her relationships at work, with her family and with prospective new partners.

Phase 7: Playing

Bella gained new respect from her peers and managers. She was asked to manage teams and had the freedom and strong sense of self to be playful at work. She built relationships with intimacy and connection and was creative in response to workplace challenges. Her personal life changed as she changed her relationships at work. She began new pursuits such as drawing and singing. She began to be more creative in designing her home as a sacred and beautiful space to nourish herself after work. Play and creativity were increasing Bella's sense of wellbeing many more times than before she began this journey.

Phase 8: Embodiment

While developing these new skills, Bella became aware of a heightened sense of intuiting and detecting people who had controlling behaviours and who were energy drainers. She sensed energy when she was with people who embodied values of respect and freedom similar to her values. She was now living out her values of freedom and self-respect and could let go of the need to control others. In turn, she could sense when she was being controlled by others and could create new boundaries of self-respect. She began to better discern the people she could be with at work and at home who appreciated each other's uniqueness. She was attracting different people into her life with ease and grace.

Phase 9: Patterning

Bella now has the skills to adapt and learn from life events. She achieved this by choosing to pause and deeply embody reflective and playful practices for self-discovery. She can now discern a deeper dimension of being able to create the success she desires and what she is doing that is a potential sabotage. She can reveal unconscious patterns in her behaviour, events and the behaviour of others. She has opened herself to the unseen, to what can be intuited through sensory, body and imaginary knowledge and to new fields of possibility. She feels like she is a different person from when we first met. She says she feels like she did when she was a child who could freely express themselves, play and be curious about life.

Whatever life events show up for Bella, she knows how to learn from them. She has ways to listen in to an inner body language, through non-rational forms, when to pay attention to the rational and the intuitive to make sense of life.

Bella's two-year journey

From		*To*
Angst over divorce	⇒	Knowing it was the right choice
Controlling, dominating parents who made her feel guilty	⇒	Adult-adult relationships with her parents built on respect
Hating being single	⇒	Loving herself and her life
Dating people who did not suit	⇒	Consciously sensing who had similar values
Dating the 'wrong' people	⇒	Becoming exclusive with a new partner
A marriage where there was disrespect	⇒	A new marriage built on solid foundations of trust
An inability to resolve conflict or shifting conflict	⇒	Understanding and loyalty
Misunderstanding emotional triggers	⇒	The opportunity to grow into her best self
A controlling boss	⇒	A supportive partner
Needing to stay in a corporate job for security	⇒	Choosing to leave the corporate life and being asked back as a consultant
Being unhappy and single	⇒	Visioning a successful life with family and fulfilment in work and creating it

Bella's life would not have become like this had she not paused and known she needed some help with how to make sense of life.

She overcame some of her greatest fears:

"Will I repeat the mistakes of my parents? Will I ever be good enough to create a successful relationship? Will I ever be good enough to stop working 80 hours a week to prove myself? Will I be successful at work and home?"

Bella has redefined success and has shifted from being a perfectionist who created stress in her life to becoming successful at making wise choices for both her personal life and her work.

In essence, Bella has become a master. She has developed her sensory and intuitive capacities and can integrate the rational with the intuitive for her success. She can:

- Integrate the sensory and intuitive with the rational
- Express her energy and emotional expression
- Exform blocks and create space for the new to emerge
- Notice blind spots and uncover the congruence or incongruence of her actions, feelings and words
- Play with movement and and synthesise new information with improvisation that fosters freedom, connection and fulfilment
- Engage with self and other non-defensively to check that her new knowledge is taking her towards her vision and aligned with her values
- Intuit unseen patterns and be open to the emergence of new possibilities that rational logic does not allow.

As Bella learnt these skills to be more successful creating her life, my life changed as well. The mentor and mentee relationship is a cooperative, interdependent process. Living and learning together.

CHOICES

The first step of any journey is to make the first choice.

Jess

I was coaching Jess recently about how to make choices that lit her up. She was experiencing a challenge with her relationship. Her boyfriend would call and say, "I'd love you to come over, but I have things to do, so I cannot spend much time with you." She would say, "Okay, it doesn't matter. I will see you soon." And she would go to his house. At the same time she would be thinking, "I want to be with you, and if I don't come over, you won't like that, so I had better say 'yes' so you know I love you." Then she would go over to his place, and just as he told her, he would be busy doing his jobs. She would sit in his house twiddling her thumbs, thinking about all of the things that she would love to be doing at her place.

In the meantime, her body would become irritated, and she would think resentful thoughts. He would notice her irritation and ask, "What's going on?" She would respond, "Nothing. Nothing's wrong."

The next minute, they would be having an argument, and it would not be the night either of them had wanted. She would leave upset. It would take a few days before they both recovered from the conflict. They had no idea why it had arisen. The tension and unresolved conflict left residue in their bodies, creating distance rather than a connection between them.

Often this is the case when saying 'yes' to something that we don't want to do or 'no' to something we want to do.

As Jess was learning how to focus on the senses in her body and how to choose on her intuition, not her logic, she began to make some changes. She rang me to tell me about a development.

"Debbie, I'm excited. My boyfriend asked me over. I asked what we were going to do and what he had to do that night. He told me he had to pack and get organised for his trip. I knew we wouldn't have time for each other, and I said, 'No, you do what you have to do tonight. I have things I want to do, and I'm going to stay at my place. You aren't going away for a few days. I'll see you tomorrow night when we have time to enjoy each other's company.'

"I was amazed at the difference it made to both him and me. I got to re-create the space in my room by moving some furniture, bringing out some of my favourite books and chill out. He got to pack and get organised in peace. We went out the next day and had a great time.

I didn't tell a white lie. I didn't have to pretend. I chose powerfully. I chose what was right for me, and it was good for our relationship at the same time. I did not make the choice based on thinking I had to do something for him so he would love me. I made it based on what I sensed that I needed and what he needed at the time."

sense an energetic connection when apart

Jess now makes powerful choices for her career and her relationships. She learnt to notice physical sensations and emotions that arise in her body. She learnt to imagine new pathways solving relationship challenges with her boss, family members, and partner. She has also learnt to understand the messages that arise from her feelings and identify what action is the best to take for her best interests.

How do you make your choices? Do you go around in circles or get stuck not knowing what to decide? Do you choose the wrong thing and have regrets, or avoid choices and feel stuck having settled for the status quo?

What if you could learn new ways to make powerful choices that align with your inner truth and heart's desire?

What if you knew how to notice what:

Lights you up

Senses and feel right, even though your thinking, rational mind tells you differently

Creates new pathways and new ways to overcome obstacles

Is not for your highest good

Is connected to a sense of your purpose in life and who you are?

The intention behind a choice

When you make a choice to 'get' others to love you or to please others, it often backfires.

When you choose what is 'right' for you, even though you imagine others may not like your choice, you create happiness and congruence for yourself and others.

Noticing when we are choosing to control the world and when we are living in cooperation with our world enables us to find a new rhythm for our lives.

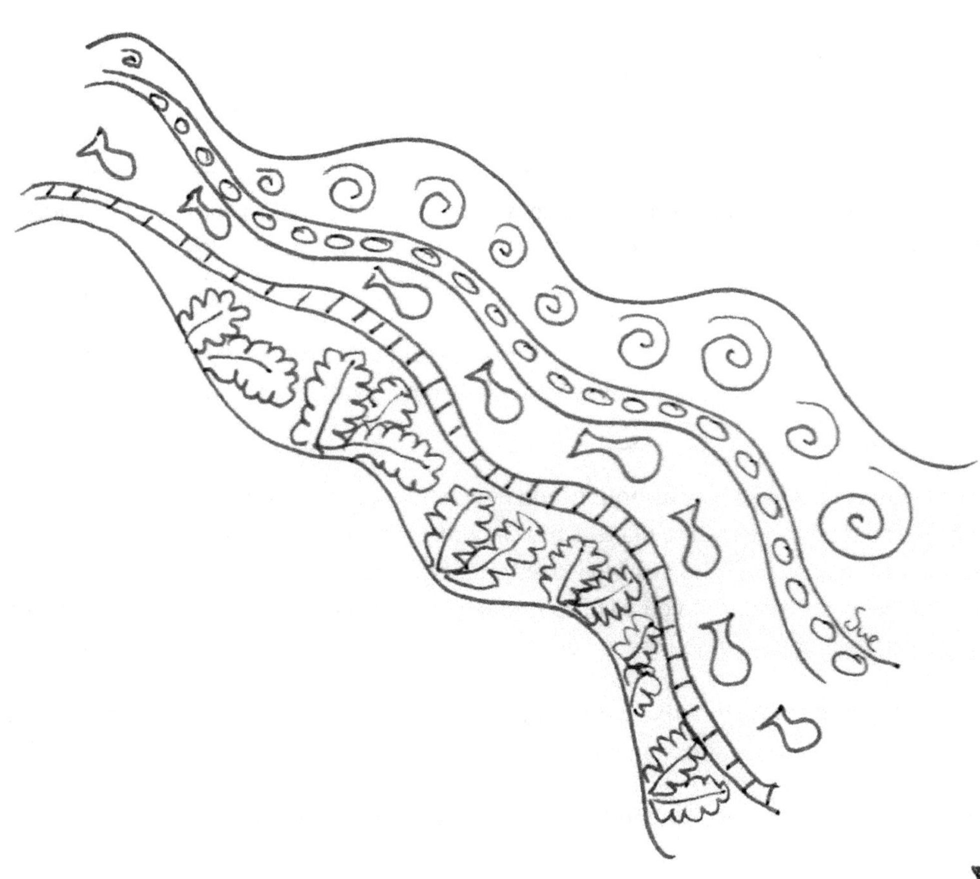

THE INVITATION

Become an explorer of your innate wisdom. Be able to choose powerfully for both the little things and the big choices in life. You are invited to:

Notice physical sensory responses in your body and movement

Activate your imagination and play with options

Understand the messages from your feelings.

In the third section of this book, there is a guide to help you explore including sensing, moving, imagining and playing to make powerful choices. If you are itching to get started now, try out the example practices below. These will create the foundations for a deeper connection with yourself as you progress through the book.

Step 1: Notice physical sensory responses in your body

Starting today, pay attention to how your physical, sensory body responds to invitations and choices. You might not be used to this, as we have been trained to think and consider our thoughts rather than what our body is telling us. So, it may take a little time to notice the messages that you have been overlooking.

Your physical, sensory body can tingle, be tense, be at ease, expansive, or tight, and can feel a range of temperature, textures, movements, energies, paralysis, feelings, aches, pains, and more.

Over the next few weeks, pay attention, and notice how your body responds with sensations and movements when asked to make a choice. While learning to deepen this knowledge, it is good to practice on small choices. How does your body respond when asked by your partner what you want for dinner; if you wish to go for a walk; what to watch on TV; which way to drive to work; what flavour ice cream, etc.?

The better you get at connecting with your inner wisdom on small things, the more powerful you will be with the big choices in life.

There are four key situations to notice your body's response to in your exploration:

YES

When you say 'yes' to something, and you know it is right for you, how does your body respond?

Notice. Pay attention. Capture the information.

Does your body tingle with excitement? Where? All over? In your heart? Does your body feel expansive and open? We all feel something different. What does 'yes' feel like for you?

NO

When you say 'no' to something, and you know this is right for you, how does your body respond?

Notice. Pay attention. Capture the information.

Does your body feel firm, closed and grounded? Where? All over? In your back? We all feel something different. What does 'no' feel like for you?

MAYBE

When you are unsure, maybe you say 'yes,' but on second thought, mean 'no,' or you say 'no' and mean 'yes'. How does your body respond?

Notice. Pay attention. Capture the information.

Does your body feel uneasy or queasy? Where? All over? In your gut? We all feel something different. What does 'maybe' feel like for you?

PRETENDING

Sometimes we pretend to want to do something and say 'yes' even though we know we want to say 'no'. Sometimes we pretend we don't want something and say 'no' even though we know we want to say 'yes'.

This happens when we are pleasing others or doing something because we believe it will make us look good, make others love us, get us a promotion, etc.

How does your body respond? Notice. Pay attention. Capture the information.

Does your body feel irritated? Where? All over? In your legs? We all feel something different. What does it feel like when you are pretending?

You will experience four different physical, sensory body and energetic responses. Learn to notice the difference. You will realise this is valuable body data for learning how to make powerful choices.

When making a choice, even if all of the rational reasons in the world point to 'yes', if you are in touch with your body's response, you can check in and see if it feels good deep in your body.

I invite you to play with this, test it out, and learn to connect with the deep sensory, energetic, and spiritual messages that arise from your body. This is one way of noticing and sensing our physical, sensory responses. Keep noticing, connecting, and practising every day of your life.

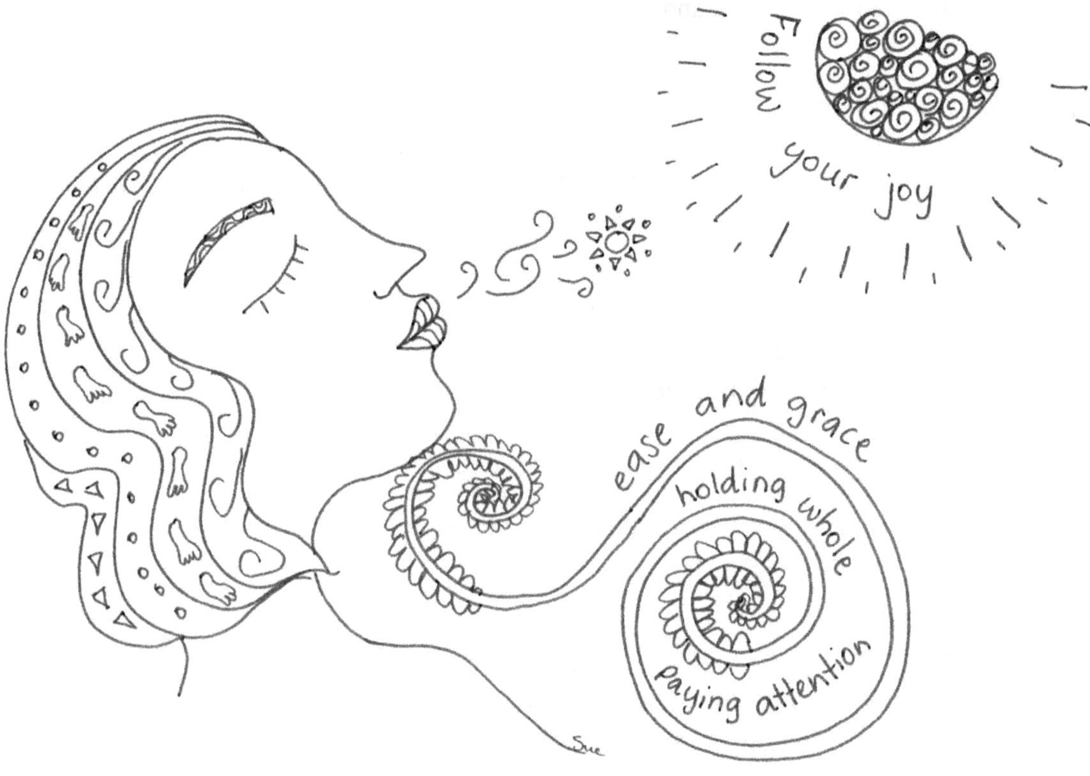

The next step is to explore different options for the choices you want to make in life.

Step 2: Activating your imagination and playing with options

Did I use the word 'play' again? Yes! Just because you are an adult, it does not mean you have to stop playing. When you were a child, you learnt the most information in the shortest possible time through playing. While you are playing, you are also:

Sensing

Feeling

Touching

Smelling

Seeing

Tasting

Hearing

Imagining

Discovering

Experimenting

So, now, I invite you to play!

Whatever choice you have to make, imagine three options. When you have your three options, I invite you to imagine you are living the consequences of that option. Imagine being in a movie, and you are writing the script of how that choice will play out in your life. Imagine the people you will meet, your physical location, what you hear yourself saying, what you hear others saying. Use all of your senses—auditory, visual, and kinaesthetic—to make that choice feel alive in your body.

Let's try an example. Imagine you are making a career choice and have an opportunity to work for another company. Two options are obvious: stay, or go. But let's imagine there are at least three options:

1. You could stay where you are currently working

2. You could work for the new company

3. You could go into business for yourself or seek out another company.

Now, play with how each choice feels in your body. Notice your body sensations when you imagine living that choice.

Option 1

Imagine staying with your current company. Walk as if you are walking to work. What do you feel? Is there a feeling of dread, contentment, unease? See what emerges from your imagination.

Option 2

Imagine working for a new company. Imagine taking that position. Walk as if you are walking into a new workplace. Sense how your body feels when you move and imagine taking that new position. What is your sensory response? Do you feel energised? Do you feel nervous? Imagine yourself as if you are in a movie, working for that company.

Option 3

Explore another choice. For example: "I'm going to leave the corporate world or employment for good, and I'm going to start my own business." Be present to your body's response. Play with walking, moving and sitting as if you are now in your own business.

What does your body feel and sense when you imagine yourself leaving your current employment and starting a new business? Do you feel excited, invigorated, enlivened, or frightened? Stay with these different emotions, feelings, and body sensations to explore them further to feel what is a 'yes' and what is a 'no' so that you get to know how your body expresses 'yes' and 'no'.

Imagining three choices

Your imagination is important in this process. When you have a choice to make, imagine all of the options fully. Practise each one. "I am going to try on being self-employed. I'm going to imagine what it's like writing a video script, and I am the main character."

Imagine leaving your current employment, having the celebration, packing up your things. Make it as real as possible and imagine it. Imagine setting up your office in your home or finding a new office. Bring it in as if you are making a video, a visual image. What would you be hearing? What would people be saying to you? What would you hear in your head? What would you be feeling?

Bring all of this into your imagination and play it out. Live it for a while to see how you feel about this choice.

Your imagination, playing, and practising are activities to learn how to choose powerfully.

Playing is an important part of making new choices and choosing powerfully. Often, we make it such hard work as if our life depended on it. You can play. You can experiment. You can figure out how much time you've got before you need to make the choice. In that amount of time, try it on, experiment, see how each choice feels. And that brings us nicely to the next topic: your feelings.

Step 3: Understanding the messages from your feelings

When you imagine your three options, you probably noticed different feelings arising. Few of us have learnt how to read and understand our feelings, so we often make choices after inaccurately listening to our feelings.

For example, perhaps you felt nervous imagining taking on a new position, so you chose to stay where you are currently employed. You thought the nervousness meant, "Do not take a risk and stay with what you know."

However, nervousness means different things for different people in different contexts.

The more you pay attention to your body's responses and notice your feelings, the more you will start to understand what your feelings are telling you in any particular situation.

Here is a brief introduction to understanding a new way to take actions based on the feelings in your body.

This is a guide. It is not prescriptive. Check yourself for the meaning of your feelings for you in your current situation. We are all different, but there are some common meanings of our feelings across cultures.

Frustration

Frustration is often related to needing to see new actions, as our old ways no longer work for us. Check that you have truly exhausted all current possibilities—imagine

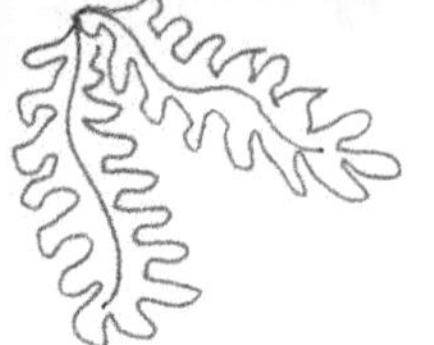

new pathways, new options, and new choices. Be creative and imagine totally new ways to understand your situation.

Anxiety, nervousness or fear

These feelings often arise from safety, security, or confidence issues. Check what you need to do to feel safe and secure about a choice. You are responsible for your safety. If you want to choose a new pathway, and you feel anxiety, check in with yourself to see if there are ways to create safety. If there are no ways to create safety, your fear or anxiety may be warning you that it is not a right choice for you.

Joy, bliss or expansiveness

Feeling joyous, blissful or expansive can often indicate a right path for us. This usually means the choice, thought, or action is right for you. Check in with yourself. Does this feel true for you? Is your body opening up to what will give you great joy? Will you take it? Are you ready to enjoy the joy, bliss and expansiveness of this choice?

Anger

Issues with respect and boundaries can create feelings of anger. Where have you let someone walk all over you? Where have you let someone take away your power? What do you need to do to restore your self-respect?

Does this mean you are angry and blaming someone for a choice you have made in the past? If you begin to make choices for yourself, how does that feel in your body? Allow the anger, which is energy, to be released in a safe way. Running, beating a cushion or yelling in the shower are safe ways to release anger. Taking action for yourself to create respect will also release the anger.

Resentment

Resentment is often related to blaming someone or yourself for something that happened in the past. This is also related to living with regret and living in the past rather than knowing you have influence over the present and your future.

Who are you blaming for your current situation? How can you take responsibility for creating your life now? Rather than blame others, see where you can take action to restore your personal power and respect your ability to make choices for yourself. See how you can focus taking action now to create a better future rather than being resentful about something that happened in the past. Learn to accept your regret and take new actions to be happy with your next choices.

Sadness

Sadness often arises from loss. What needs to be honoured, cared for, and loved? How can you allow yourself to feel sadness at lost opportunities or the loss of something? What can you do to love and care for yourself to allow the sadness to flow through you? Feel the sadness and let it be released.

There is much to learn from your feelings. Beyond this brief introduction to understanding the messages from your feelings, there are more ways to access your inner wisdom so you can make powerful choices in your life.

Noticing—your energy, your multiple 'selves', your inner crew

Sensing—your body sensing what it needs and knows

Moving—your body tapping into intelligence through movement

Intuiting—your higher awareness of patterns and spiritual guidance.

NOTICING

The range of what we think and do is limited
by what we fail to notice. And because we fail
to notice that we fail to notice, there is little we
can do to change until we notice how failing
to notice shapes our thoughts and deeds.
– R. D. Laing

What are you noticing right now?

If I ask you to find an object that is green right now, it is likely that you will start noticing everything that is green. A moment before, all the green objects were a part of the background along with many other objects.

We can only focus on so many things at any one time, but what if we have become so accustomed to looking at certain things in known comfortable places that we are missing the very things we are looking for?

Noticing only in the familiar, comfortable places is like looking in the light under a lamppost for your keys, even though you dropped them in another place where it is dark. When asked why you aren't looking where you dropped them, you answer, "Oh, it is too dark over there." We can spend countless hours looking in the wrong place and going nowhere.

Most of us have been taught to focus, to want to develop goals and achieve defined outcomes. What we have not been encouraged to do is purely notice what is going on around us, collect that information, turn it into patterns and make sense of it in ways that help us live our lives well.

Noticing is different from being outcome-focused. Being outcome-focused usually means knowing what you want, pre-determining it and taking the actions to achieve exactly what you have determined.

Noticing turns this upside down. Noticing is being childlike, curious and interested in what might turn up newly. Even though we are making judgements about things all the time, when we stay in an open and noticing frame of mind, we are likely to find new patterns of meaning. By judging something as right or wrong, we close off our options too early, therefore, new patterns of meaning and creativity are closed off.

Right and wrong, bad and good, all judgements are not necessarily helpful when we want to be open to learning new information in order to access new wisdom.

Life is what it is. We can learn to notice things as they are and they are not.

There are many things we can notice.

Relationships and behaviour:	how what we do and say affects another person, and how a person, location or event affects our behavior
Language:	how words affect our physical body, the beliefs we have about ourselves, and the actions we choose
Energy:	how it shifts and changes depending on who we are with, what we are doing, thinking and sensing, and where we are
Thoughts:	how our thoughts change our energy
Physical space:	how it affects how we feel, our energy and our safety
Animals:	how we feel when in contact with an animal
Plants:	what we feel when in contact with plants
Earth:	what we notice when we have our feet on the earth, sand, bitumen or concrete.

These are a few pointers. What we can notice is endless. The exercises in the third section of this book will give you some ways to take notice of your life and learn something new.

In the meantime, you can start playing with a new, soft, curious focus—noticing is being curious, like a scientist who experiments with the effects of combining different compounds and being surprised at what is found. Noticing is being observant and interested without judgement. Noticing is being playful like an artist who plays with different colours, textures and brush strokes until magic appears. Noticing is like dancers who improvise, weaving in and out with each other until they synchronise together in a newly discovered dance form.

What do you notice as you go about your day?

What magic do you find?

Locations have memory

I drive past a busy cross section, and each time I remember the accident I had over 30 years ago, I cringe. I drive on.

Words have memory

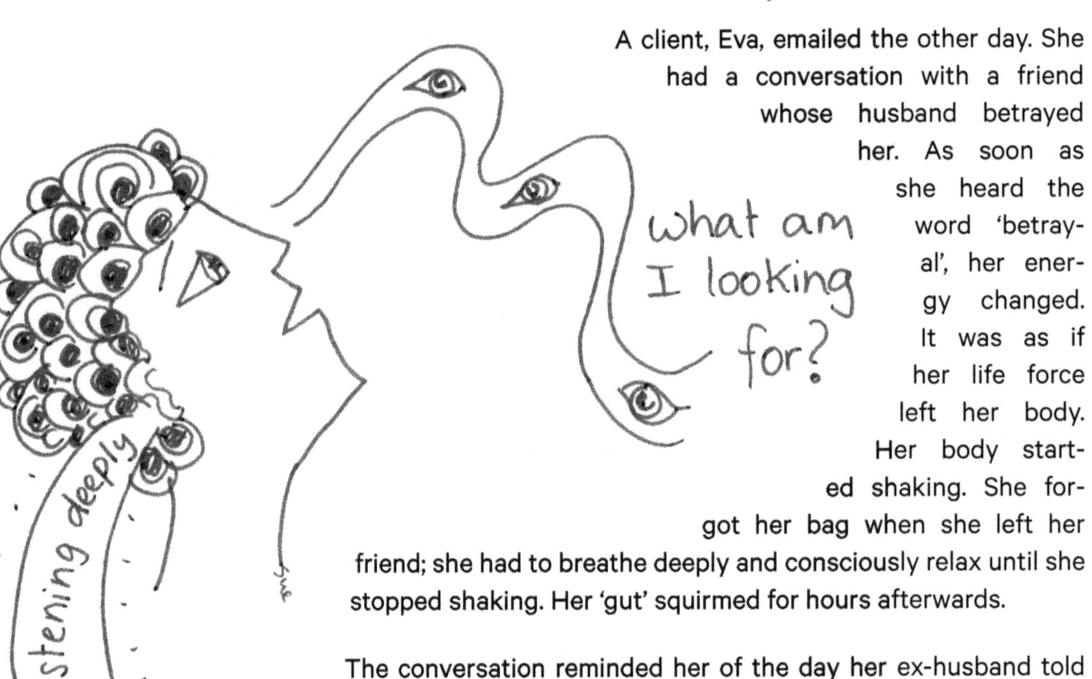

A client, Eva, emailed the other day. She had a conversation with a friend whose husband betrayed her. As soon as she heard the word 'betrayal', her energy changed. It was as if her life force left her body. Her body started shaking. She forgot her bag when she left her friend; she had to breathe deeply and consciously relax until she stopped shaking. Her 'gut' squirmed for hours afterwards.

The conversation reminded her of the day her ex-husband told her he was having an affair. The word 'betrayal' had an energetic and physical memory in her body; it was not a thought separated from her body.

Words and our physicality

Spoken language evolved from our experiences, but today we read and listen to words from people on the other side of the world, from places we have never visited and about activities we have never physically done. While we have the intelligence to make sense of words through comparing them to our similar experiences, the further away we are from our lived experience, the more potential there is for misunderstanding. The closer we are to a face to face experience, where we have the aid of our physical body, and visual and sensory acuity, the better we can understand one another.

Words have a physical response. Our preoccupation with abstract theory and logic has contributed to a disconnect between what we say, feel and do. We have acted as if words are not connected to our body, as if they are out there in the world and do not affect our emotions and sensory experience of being alive. Descriptive, emotive, symbolic words evoke the physical connection and stir our very being in ways that abstract language does not.

The new trend to regain the art of storytelling is recovering the physical connection between words and both our felt and imaginal experience. This is recovering our connection between making meaning and being stirred emotionally, physically, and energetically while making sense of the world. Storytelling helps us sense our disconnection and our connection with our truth.

Walking our talk

We often say someone is walking their talk, or not walking their talk. In essence, the words someone says are either in alignment with their actions or they are disconnected and out of alignment.

We can sense and feel there is a disconnect even if we are unsure of what it is that we are sensing.

Sensing a disconnect often leads us to being suspicious of a person.

We lose trust with someone who uses words that are not congruent with their physical presence and the actions they take.

When we lose trust, we distance ourselves from those we do not trust.

When we distance ourselves from others, we lose the very sense of belonging to a community that is one of our basic human needs.

We become selective about what we will say and what we won't.

While we think we are doing this to protect ourselves, it often has the opposite effect.

We lose the opportunity for connection.

We then suffer from alienation, abandonment, loneliness and various depths of stress and depression.

We can choose to stop going down this pathway of protecting ourselves in a way that leads to isolation, or not.

Once we make the first choice, there is a second and third choice

The second choice, to resolve our own inner conflict and settle into our truth, is an imperative.

The third choice is whether to speak to the person we are relating to about what we are seeing that is incongruent. The ability to discern whether to speak up or not is dependent on many elements.

Do you have a long-term relationship with the person?

Has the person invited feedback?

Can you resolve your inner congruence without speaking up about another person's incongruence?

This book is focused on our own inner dialogue and how to create our inner freedom. The capacity to speak with another in this way is the subject matter of another book, however, in essence being aware of some of the following principles will help you discover the art of talking about blind spots.

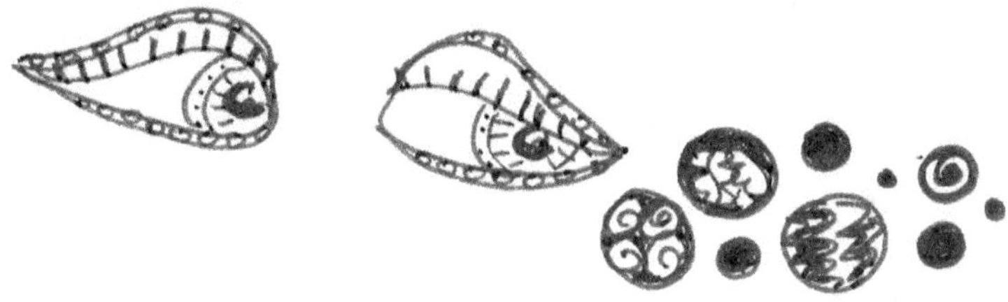

Blind spots in another person

Learning to choose whether to disclose the confusion when someone speaks or acts incongruently is an art. If we share what we notice, the person we are speaking with is likely to become defensive, as they have not seen what we can see. There is an art in creating the safety between each other to have conversations about the unseen. The best way is to have an attitude of curiosity: "I noticed x, did you?" Curiosity and exploration, rather than an attitude of one being right and the other wrong, lay a foundation for openness, new discoveries and new connections.

Noticing incongruence in others is only half of the story. We, too, have areas where we are incongruent and we are blind to our incongruence. We all have blind spots. There are two major ways to discover our blindness:

1. Build trusting relationships where we can be curious and honest with one another
2. Become competent at sensing our own disconnection when we say or take actions that are out of alignment.

This takes us into the area of sensory awareness, which is the subject of the next chapter. To start this conversation let's take the time to notice our energy.

The energy of incongruence

There is energy attached to the incongruence between what we believe, what we say and what we do. This energy is either contained within our body or explodes at unexpected times. The energy impacts our lives without us even knowing. It takes more energy to maintain anger or a frown than it does to let it go, or to smile. But we fight our incongruence, pretending to be somebody we are not, covering up what we really believe and feel.

When we hold onto an incongruence, we are likely to have an energy of pushing or pulling on others. We will be needy for something that we are not giving ourselves or we will push away from people who want to give us what we really need.

Holding on

I always remember my father's laugh, a laugh on the outside and pain on the inside. No matter how much suffering he endured, he would always keep it to himself, never complain, and smile. The trauma he experienced early in life in World War II was never released. The suffering was contained in his body and caused much pain. In his 70s, he was told by a medical specialist, "If we had treated you for post-traumatic stress, we would not have had to operate on your back."

This was too late for my father. Three operations later and he suffered even more physical pain and with the additional consequence of limited physical movement.

When Dad had a car accident at 60, the trauma held in his body was disturbed. He could no longer contain the tension and his body fell to pieces after holding his post-traumatic stress from World War II in his body for 50 years. In the 1950s he did not have a counsellor to help him release the trauma from war.

Men were told not to surrender to their emotions, not to grieve or cry, just as they told their children. I am a child of the 60s. Even though I was female, it was still not seen to be appropriate to share feelings, to share a fear or to share unspeakable events that occurred behind closed doors in families. We buttoned up. The energy of our traumas does not go away; it stays sleeping in our bodies until awakened by some event in life, and then the energy slips out in unpredictable ways.

Triggers

Have you ever felt that someone presses your buttons or triggers behaviour that is not normally you? We may burst into anger, sadness or fear that we cannot explain. Unconsciously, an experience reminds us of something that happened in the past. It is these experiences that open up the cracks to release the energy that has been contained. It is these experiences that are a gift to release unresolved issues from the past. The more we hang on to unresolved issues from the past, the more we are incongruent and stuck in a self-defeating cycle.

There is a way to get unstuck: learn to notice your energy.

We experience our energy differently when we are aligned with what we say and what we do, than when we say something and do the opposite. When we are not living our truth, we create inner tension. This inner tension is like a constant itch. It will not go away until the energy is released and we live our truth.

Living our truth creates ease and freedom.

Today, my father could have seen a somatic therapist to release the trauma from his body. He could have learnt how to self-care and to release tension at the time of any event in his

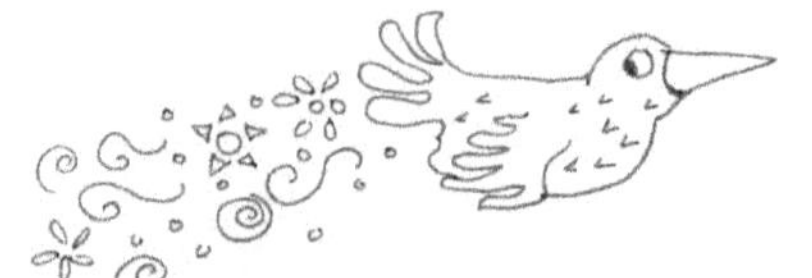

life when experiencing trauma. This would have enabled him to return to a natural state of being free from tension on a daily basis.

Peter Levine, in his book *Waking the Tiger: Healing Trauma: The Innate Capacity to Transform Overwhelming Experiences* (Levine, 1997)[11], shares an incident when he was walking along a footpath and knocked down by a car. He recalls he had enough consciousness after the accident to tell his rescuers not to restrain his body. He believes that because his body was allowed to go through a natural process of shutting down, shaking, quivering and moving in a natural state, he was not left with residual trauma in his body. He healed quickly.

Our natural instincts

As a human being, it is a natural instinct to protect ourselves when threatened emotionally, psychologically, financially, or physically. We have the capacity to 'leave our bodies' and to disconnect from our feelings and senses to protect ourselves from an emotional state of pain and suffering. Escaping our bodies in times of trauma is a natural protective mechanism, for humans and other animals. It is known that when prey animals, such as deer, finally accept their fate when being attacked by a predator, they will go into a state similar to amnesia. Scientists believe it must numb the pain of dying. If the lion retreats and the deer returns to safety, its natural instinct is to release stress through shaking its body, and the deer's body returns to a contented state. This is the deer's natural instinct to stop, sense safety and shake out the trauma of the chase. When back in safety, the deer returns to being relaxed and grazes, while still maintaining its senses to be alert for the next predator in its territory.

Animals in the wild have maintained their natural instincts. Humans, on the other hand, have numbed them down.

"We have become sanitised and de-animalised."
- David Abram[12]

11 Peter Levine, the author of Waking the Tiger: Healing Trauma: The Innate Capacity to Transform Overwhelming Experiences (Levine, 1997)

12 David Abram, Becoming Animal: An Earthly Cosmology,

If we feel stress, the simple act of shaking and moving our body can shift our body into a state of ease. In the third section of this book, there are exercises to notice your energy, release energy and create the space within yourself to sense freedom. When our body is free, creativity arises. When it is tense, we block our energy and creativity.

We have disconnected with our bodies, the earth, nature and our ancient senses. We stop and control our natural body and animal instincts. We forget to come back home into our bodies when we are no longer under threat, or no longer reading abstract material or working with technology. Humans have overridden many of our natural protective responses, even those that benefit us.

On the other hand, there are natural instincts that are beneficial to overcome for living in a diverse society. Social scientists say that it is a natural instinct for us to gather in likeness, in tribes, whether that be gender, culture, religion or ability. In earlier centuries, tribes of likeness dominated others to make them like themselves. But we could not have expanded unless we learnt to live with differences. We would have continued to have wars to oppress groups different from ourselves, and the world would not be as populated. Now most of us live in cities rich with people from many different cultures, religions, sexual orientations and ways of creating a family. We can choose to overcome the instinct to gather in likeness and learn how to empathise and accept people who are different from us. Consciously choosing to be aware of our biases is both an ongoing challenge and an imperative.

The age we live in has been referred to as the Consumer Age, the Information Age and the Digital Age, among others. Philosopher Professor Richard Kearney[13] has another view on our current age that seems not just descriptive, but diagnostic. He refers to our modern era as the Age of Excarnation—the 'Out of Body Age'. The phrase perfectly captures the unseen and unspoken normal way in which we go about our daily affairs. Day in, day out, we predominantly live in a mode of being in which we are out of touch with our bodies. As a

13 Professor Richard Kearney, https://richardmkearney.com/

result, the world exists for us more often as an idea than as a felt reality. We are preoccupied elsewhere. Our bodies are giving us the signals of stress and overwhelm, giving us cues to change what we are doing and thinking that are disconnecting us from our humanity, but we have forgotten the language of our bodies and do not hear the cues.

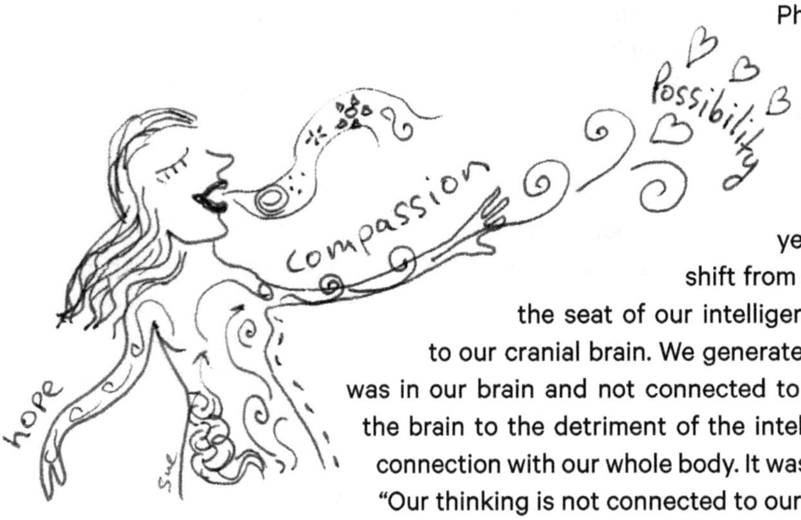

Phillip Shepherd, in his book *New Self, New World: Recovering Our Senses in the Twenty-First Century*[14], says that it was approximately 1400 years ago that we made a shift from our gut and pelvic area as the seat of our intelligence, to our heart and then to our cranial brain. We generated a belief that intelligence was in our brain and not connected to our body. We focused on the brain to the detriment of the intelligence that arises from a connection with our whole body. It was Rene Descartes who said, "Our thinking is not connected to our bodies or our emotions."

We know now this is not true. Our brains create meaning through connection to the intelligence in our bodies, our senses and every cell in our body. Intelligence arises from an inter-connection with our mind, body and energy and the world in which we live. Dr Bruce Lipton says in his book, *Biology of Belief: Unleashing the Power of Consciousness, Matter & Miracles*[15], that there is intelligence in every cell in our body. Our physiology and well-being are connected to our beliefs. Words affect our physical state; our physical state affects what we think. We are an inter-connected system of thoughts, feelings, senses and energy interacting with the environment and other people's thoughts, feelings, senses and energy.

While this is generally accepted by modern society, our collective belief system is still recovering from Descartes' view that thought, feeling, senses and energy are not connected. When we believe our thoughts are separate from our body, we live 'in our heads', imagining our worlds and disconnecting from our feelings and senses, which results in anxiety. The very suppression and avoidance of sensing our physical state is not healthy.

Since we were small, many of us were told not to cry, not to feel grief, to control being angry, to stop talking about how we feel, as if logic and reason are more important than what we feel.

---

14 Phillip Shepherd, New Self, New World: Recovering Our Senses in the Twenty-First Century
15 Dr. Bruce Lipton, Biology of Belief: Unleashing the Power of Consciousness, Matter & Miracles,

This creates a false disconnection. This disconnection is the source of much anxiety, stress, tension and conflict.

In our society, we have disengagement at work, we have addictions to substances, products and behaviours, and we have depression, anxiety and conflict.

But there is a gift in every challenge. The challenges today of stress, conflict and disengagement in the workplace and at home are pulling us back into our bodies and towards what makes us more human.

Evolution is occurring.

While we have forces pulling us out of our body, our response is to compensate. Even though we may not say our problem is disconnection with our body, we are pulled into activities that take us out of our mind and back into our body. The overwhelming trends in the following activities are all pulling us into our bodies and our humanity:

Meditation

Yoga

Healthful, natural food

Body therapy

Exercise

Massage

Kinesiology

Storytelling

Colouring in books

Dance

Nature.

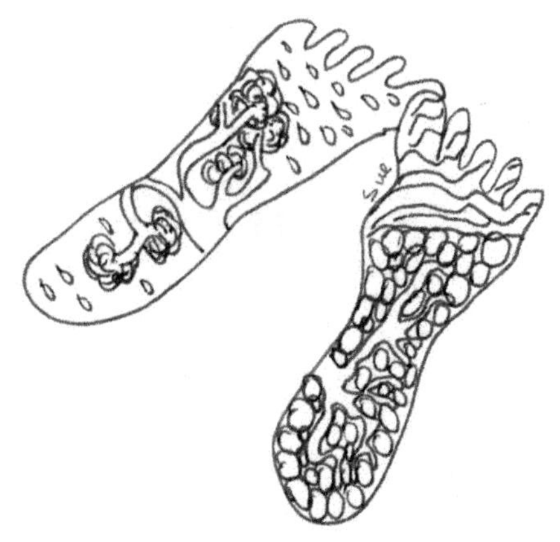

Some of these activities provide temporary relief from the alienation that we experience when disconnected from our whole selves, however, to live our lives as fully embodied people we need to aim for embodiment throughout all our waking and sleeping moments—not just to experience being in our body while taking a class.

I pursued Buddhist practices for some time. I was most drawn to the work of Thich Nat Hahn, *Peace Is Every Step: The Path of Mindfulness in Everyday Life* [16], which made available processes of mindfulness in daily life. I learnt that I did not have to sit cross-legged like a yogi for hours on end. I learnt to be present in my experience in every step, in every moment. I practised such things as walking meditation, washing the dishes meditation and having a shower meditation.

These practices were one of the pathways that restored my whole-bodied connection. While there are substantial benefits to meditation, I needed other whole bodied experiences to help me understand the messages from my physical sensory body. Meditation invites us to notice and watch the impermanence of what we feel and not be attached. My search to understand physical sensory and imaginal experiences like a message, took me to a different dimension of understanding and caring for myself.

Listening to the body as a language enables me to understand in ways that I did not find from meditation.

Much of the work currently written about the body has more to do with the food we need to eat, our physical well-being and emotional well-being. In this book, I invite us to go further.

The connection with our body senses, which include physical and emotional well-being, can connect us to a natural source of what I call 'innate body wisdom', which is primed to return us to a healthy state of being. If we keep overriding this innate body wisdom, we turn off our communication channel to what makes us feel alive, what food makes us healthy, what thoughts contribute to our well-being. We turn off the tap that is the source of our creativity. We turn off access to the energy that nourishes our soul. We turn off the tap of energy that

16 Thich Nat Hahn, Peace Is Every Step: The Path of Mindfulness in Everyday Life, Bantam Books, 1991

sustains loving relationships. We turn off a vast body of wisdom that is innate.

We are living in a time where we are shaking off the shackles of being controlled by authoritarian power. Where once we handed over our power to the church, to the aristocracy, to teachers, we have lost trust in many of these established power structures. As we have become more educated we have looked more to science to provide us with answers than the church.

In this transition, there is something still fundamental that we are doing, which is transferring power to someone else.

I know we are deeply indebted to scientists who conduct research and have discovered incredible new knowledge that have made advances in our health and the ways we construct housing, grow food and much more.

However, I muse over science reports like these:

"science says walking in nature is good for us"[17]

"scientists discover we have a magnetic 6th sense to detect something we can not see"[18]

"science discovers our skin sends messages to our brain"

Whilst on the one hand, I find it immensely interesting and liberating that we are finding out this knowledge.

On the other hand if we turn to our senses as a source of communication, we instinctively "know" these things.

If we go for a walk and feel good breathing the air and moving our bodies, it puzzles me why we would not do more of that? We seem to wait for external authorities to tell us what is good for us. Once we know from an authority outside ourselves, we can rationalise going for a walk every day, because someone has told me so.

17 http://www.pnas.org/content/112/28/8567.abstract

18 http://www.collective-evolution.com/2016/07/07/scientists-discover-that-humans-have-a-magnetic-6th-sense-to-detect-something-we-cant-even-see/

To me, it seems like we keep finding another source of authority over our lives, and another and another. It has been so ingrained in our culture to defer to somebody else.

What about our own inner authority?

What would happen if we were our own scientists? We used our own experience, our observations, feelings and senses as the basis for our own research. We go for a walk regularly as it makes us feel alive, so we choose to do more of that. Then we read the benefits of walking. Science informs us what we are doing is even better than what we thought. Wonderful! But, if we do something and it does not feel right and science or another authority tells us it is, why would we want to override our own inner wisdom?

Does it matter, whether the science comes first or our own experiential knowledge comes first? Perhaps this is a chicken and an egg story. However, our school, society and work systems do ingrain us into trusting those who have more perceived power and credibility.

When we do listen to those who we believe have more credibility without checking with our own experience it is easy for us to lay blame, to walk away and look for another source of authority to find the answers we are seeking.

What if we learn from our experience, learn to trust our inner authority, check in with information available from others and then make our own powerful choices based on what is right for us. Would we get better at making choices that bring us to our own states of well being? Would we get better at making choices that create more human centred workplaces?

My invitation is to learn to trust our body and our experiences and become our own scientists.

Words arise from our physical, emotional, imaginal and energetic experiences. When we hear and read words they are interpreted within our body, mind, energy. The more disconnected we are from our body the more disengaged we are with the spoken or written word. At the same time words that are abstract are difficult for us to relate to our experience and we turn off.

The current resurgence in the art of storytelling is enabling us to connect the spoken and written word to our body, emotion, physicality and experience. We are "touched" and "moved" to take action. Scientists and Managers are just two groups of people who are re-learning how to share ideas with stories so people connect to their experience, the ideas and the speaker.

In Melbourne, Australia, a Manager, Michael was concerned that productivity in his team was in decline. He had attempted to give the facts, figures, graphs and statistics to his team to tell them what they needed to do to increase productivity.

There was no change.

He then asked them for their ideas and built relationships with them seeking out how they thought the Unit could improve.

There was no change.

He then went to a storyteller who helped him find a story in his life that people could relate to and would enable them to want to take the action to do both the mundane tasks in the business as well as the juicy work.

He remembered a story of how he had turned a problem of eating brussel sprouts into a game.

He remembered a story, when he was a child, of how his Mother demanded that he eat brussel sprouts. He would leave them until the end of the meal, but in doing so he was always slow at eating a meal and he did not enjoy dinner time. He turned this into a game of eating his brussel sprouts first. This meant he could savour all the food that he loved and enjoy his dinner and time with his family. He shared this story with his staff and asked his staff if they too could eat their brussel sprouts at the beginning of the week and then have the rest of the time to do all the work they loved.

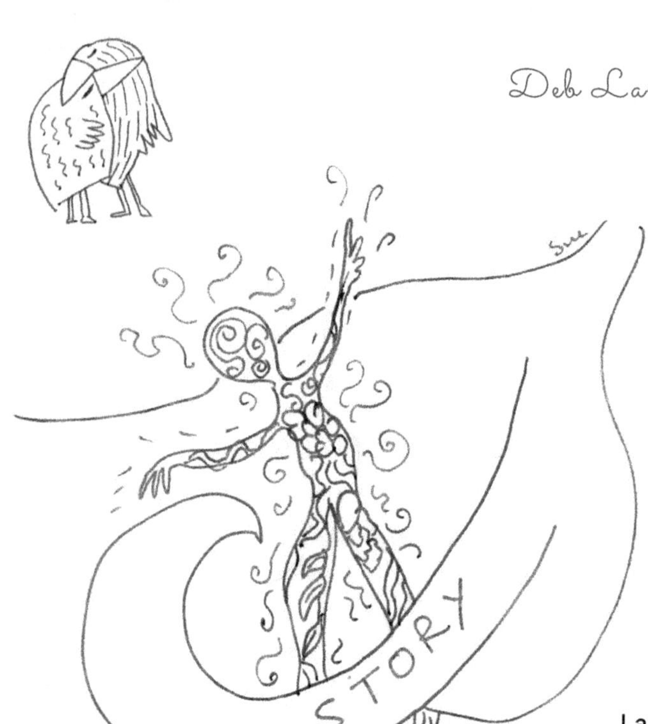

People changed and the mundane but important tasks were done.

Story is one way to reconnect to our natural inner wisdom and our connection to our body. There is an inner body language that talks to us through our senses, images and energy that is primed to nudge us towards our well-being. These cues are knocking on our door.

I am not a neuroscientist, a nutritionist or a medical practitioner. This book is written from the perspective of a lifelong educator who believes we have learnt to ignore our body intelligences, and that we can turn on the switch to reconnect the benefits of thinking with our sensory, emotional, imaginal, energetic and intuitive intelligences.

It was Howard Gardner in *Frames of Mind, The Theory of Multiple Intelligences*[19] who first wrote about intelligence in our whole body. His work affected the approach teachers took towards children who had a natural aptitude in music, dance or drawing. He helped teachers become aware that these are modes of intelligence and are different from the standard cognitive intelligence that is the basis of IQ tests. Gardner's work highlights the gifts of our multiple intelligences. We do not have to be the world's best singer, dancer or musician to enhance our life through our multiple intelligences.

Connection with more of ourselves enhances our:

Everyday sense of ourselves

Overall well-being

Communication with others

Energy for the things that matter in our life and work

Creativity in generating solutions that are for our good

Overall 'joie de vivre'.

19 Howard Gardner, Frames of Mind, The Theory of Multiple Intelligences

The more our workplaces, educational institutions, communities and family units are designed for human beings to thrive, the more we can overcome the plethora of stress and modern-day malaise that is adversely affecting our lives. By nurturing humans as whole beings with needs related to our physical, emotional, intellectual and energetic well-being, the more we will address the afflictions of the modern workplace—disengagement, conflict, high turnover, absenteeism, low morale, stress and depression.

Our whole body intelligence is accessible to all of us; it is not only for those who may have a natural aptitude towards a specifically gifted intelligence.

The wisdom of our body is latent. It has been turned off as our cultural beliefs have prioritised developing intelligence by thinking logically over sensory, energetic and intuitive forms of intelligence.

The intuitive mind is a sacred gift and
the rational mind the servant. We have
created a society that honours the
servant and has forgotten the gift.
—Albert Einstein

With the evolution of a new awareness of the intelligence in our body, a new language is surfacing, a language that is waiting to be deciphered by each of us when we turn inwards to listen to our body.

Our over-thinking mind rests when we turn to feel, sense and intuit our awareness with all of the rich diversity of senses that we have been gifted.

I do not want us to throw the baby out with the bathwater. Our inner body language (wisdom) from the inside out gives us information that we do not uncover by thinking alone. Our

sensory language from the inside out guides us to make choices for our well-being. This is a conscious whole-bodied sensing with a lighter focus than methodical, outcome-focused problem-solving of a rational, logical regime.

There is another way to reconnect with our whole selves and learn to trust the intelligence in our body, mind and energy, which is simpler and more joyful than we could imagine.

Noticing energy

As I get older, I am aware of what gives me energy. I sense how to take care of myself in ways that make my energy flow better than it has in all of my life. It has taken much, much more than just good food and exercise, which is what most people focus on: their physical health.

I have let go of relationships, activities and thoughts that drain me. I choose to do the activities that give me a sense of aliveness; I have thoughts that give me meaning; I feel connected to my purpose and have a sense of joy for my existence. Even when I am still or quiet, I feel the energy within me and in the source of life itself. When I feel sad or anxious I have ways to be present to what is and understand. I have much excitement about the projects I am creating and everything is flowing. It wasn't always like this!

What about you? How is your energy for living and creating? Have you ever thought about where your energy comes from? Where does it go? Is there a finite amount of energy that you have each day, and when it is gone, you just have to plug in and get filled up like a car with petrol or recharged from an external power source?

We are born with boundless energy. Watch a child play, move, twist, stretch, roll, stop, start, make sounds, touch—they are constantly on the move and absorbed in whatever is in the present moment.

Have you noticed how sometimes you are so absorbed and passionate about what you are doing, you are up all day and night, you feel happy and content and the energy and creativity keep on streaming through you? Have you wondered whether this could be the norm? Or did you think it was just because you were excited about a project, a holiday or some one-off event?

We humans have tended to let go of our basic instincts and become immune to what our bodies are telling us. We have learnt to rely on other people for our answers and look outside ourselves for our source of energy, peace and happiness.

The good news is we can learn to listen to our bodies, access our inner wisdom and connect to an unlimited source of energy.

Patterns of energy

It is good to know what gives you energy to enjoy life. Start noticing your energy in daily activities.

Do you know what you are doing when you have boundless energy and when you are running on empty?

Is it when you are with certain people and not others?

I have some friends who I love being with as we all respect our boundaries, we listen to one another and share in each other's challenges and successes. When I am with these people, I have lots of energy.

I also have friends who I now see less of, or not at all, as I noticed when I was with them I seemed to be doing all the listening. I was always listening to their problems, helping them with their issues in life, encouraging them in their pursuits and doing jobs for them. Over time, I started noticing my energy drop when I would see my friend's name appear on my phone. I was losing energy for the conversations. At first, I would see if I could make the conversations shorter but I was still basically 'giving myself up' to the other's person's needs and not looking after myself.

Some of you will be saying, "But I am a kind person, I want to help others. I don't want to be selfish."

Exactly!

There is great confusion between knowing when we are selfish, when we need to give to ourselves, when to self-care and when we are giving away our power and energy to our partner, family or friends.

There is a difference between being selfish, being selfless and self-care.

Whether we are leading our life, our families, or leading people in workplaces and communities, when we learn to exform, we can gain greater clarity about our behaviour and the effect on ourselves and others.

When we exform, we are more open to sensory awareness of our energy and our emotions and being able to shift from states of anxiety and tension to well-being.

Exformation empties.

When we are empty, not just of thoughts (only we are never empty), we also need to empty our emotions and energy. When stuck energy is released, we can then sense clarity about relationships that are mutually satisfying and relationships that take away our energy and are controlling.

In this section, I will share three different ways of behaving. Being selfish, being selfless, and practising self-care and care of duty towards others. We may throw about the words selfish, selfless and self-care, but don't forget these are visceral experiences. They are not words alone experienced theoretically through our mind—they are lived, experienced in our body.

Do we know what it is like to sense being selfish? If we do, we are more likely to want to avoid acting in ways that are selfish than if we just think about the word as a concept. We would also be tuned to the sensory experience of others who we are overriding, taking from and exploiting—that is, being selfish.

We may understand the concept of being selfish but when we learn to connect with our body, we are open to gaining messages to understand the beliefs at the root of our behaviour. When we understand those beliefs at a visceral level, if they do not serve us we are more likely to exform them and enter into a sense of being that is self-care.

Selfish energy and behaviour are leading our lives when we are expecting others around us to do everything for us with little concern about anyone else's interests. We are likely to have an inability to share. A two-year-old does not know how to share until they experience the satisfaction of sharing and being connected to another versus the tension of taking from others and resulting in conflict. Many adults, including leaders, have an underdeveloped sense of being selfish within their body as well as an underdeveloped sense of the impact of one's selfishness on others. They literally cannot sense another person's senses. The capacity for humans to sense and understand others is pivotal to our survival as a human species.

Selfish behaviour is 'taking' behaviour. This behaviour drains and exhausts others. People who have not learnt to sense the impact of their behaviour on someone else are likely to deny that their behaviour is having any impact on others. The behaviour is in their blind spot.

If you, the reader, receive feedback that your behaviour is selfish, my suggestion is to be curious, breathe into your body and sense what emerges from your body and keep breathing. Refrain from speaking and defending yourself. If possible, in a non-defensive manner, ask what is the behaviour and the impact on others. Stay curious like an explorer. Discover what someone else can see.

Often selfish behaviour is due to being needy. When we have a disconnect between our thoughts and our body we are unable to sense the connection between what it is that we need and how we can give that to ourselves. When we stay in our heads, we are unlikely to sense the unmet emotional, psychological, physical, spiritual and relationship needs that we have. We are more likely to manifest reasons why others 'should' give into our needs and provide us with what we want, rather than sensing that we need to give something to ourselves. Instead we pull on others to give us what we need and take from others. Selfish behaviour is exhausting for others and the selfish person is never fulfilled as no one can give them what will satisfy them, which is usually self-love and self-worth.

If you find people pulling away from you, or find it hard to maintain friendships, people may be responding to your neediness. Be honest. Ask yourself whether you are giving yourself what you need, so that when you spend time with friends, you can share your life, not pull on others to meet your needs. At work if people turn away from you, it is time to sense what it is that you need to give yourself and learn to have empathy with another and practise mutual reciprocity.

When we sense how to self-care, we can give ourselves what we need emotionally, psychologically, physically, spiritually, creatively and relationally without taking any of those things from others. We ooze contentment and happiness and we are great people to be with as we have clear boundaries. We do not give ourselves away for love and approval; we do not take energy or time from others as we have learnt to sense being kind to ourselves.

Appreciative love is when we can give love in a multitude of ways without controlling what others give us. We are freely loving and supporting another person with either gifts, acts of service, emotional kindness, empathy, touch and companionship, and there is enjoyment and appreciation in the relationship.

Leadership and followship

A leader in a workplace or community who has a great sense of self-care can be present for others and allow others to shine. There is not the need to take over to look good or to maintain credibility. There is not the need to distance ourselves from others. We know how to create safe kind boundaries of respect. We can share a leadership and followship exchange. This is the style of leadership that is needed in today's organisations where people want freedom, autonomy, responsibility and creativity in their career. The ability to give permission to others to step up as appropriate based on their expertise and interest marks the qualities of a deeply connected person who can maintain their credibility while others lead. I write more specifically on this topic in a book dedicated to leadership and followship.

Selfless

There is another pattern of behaviour related to being selfless. These are the people who work all hours to please their boss as they cannot say no. They do anything for their partners to be loved. While being selfless may look as if it is an honourable behaviour, there is a twist. In a similar way to the selfish person, the sense of the selfless person is that they cannot give to themselves. To get what they need in the way of love, approval and recognition, they feel a need to give up their needs for others. This behaviour leaves the selfless person exhausted. They often say, "What about me?" But they do not know how to sense when to say no, when to say yes and when to self-care. When they are so exhausted from giving to others, they expect someone to give them something, and when they don't, they become resentful. No one expects they are supposed to give anything back. The selfless person often unconsciously expects something in return.

Once again, we can talk about these behaviours in theory and action, but it is when we feel, sense and connect our behaviour with our thoughts and feelings that we can transform limiting behaviours. Until then, we are either blind or we are theoretical which does not result in actual change.

Are you a kind, generous, person who thinks you have to give to others to be liked and loved yourself? I was selfless in my ex-defacto relationship. It did not matter how much emotional and financial support I gave to my ex-defacto partner, it was never enough. He exploited my kindness and generosity and I became exhausted from his unquenchable thirst for taking. I learnt the hard way that it is important to self-love and self-care and not to take responsibility for other people. This does not mean that I have become selfish. I still give my labour, love and kindness generously where I feel I want to, where it is needed and I feel appreciated for doing so. The difference is I detect very early when I am being taken for granted, exploited, manipulated and intimidated and can lovingly create a boundary for myself.

Being selfless is not good for anyone. It often results in giving away your power and your sense of self.

Do you know how to sense the need for self-care in your body?

Sensing power within yourself and others enable us to realise when we are giving away our power, when we are within our power and when someone is taking away our power.

What does giving your power away mean?

It means that when someone asks for something, you give it to them regardless of whether it is in your best interests.

It means that even if you are not asked for anything, you see what can be done and you take care of someone else, or you shoulder the responsibility for the relationship, finances and acts of service.

What could you be asked to give away? Any number of things:

Your values and beliefs

Your integrity

Your time

Your work

Your service

Your body

Your money

Your self-respect.

You might ask, but why would anyone willingly give up those things?

For love? For approval? For reward?

We all need love and approval. It would be fantastic if we were born to parents who knew how to love themselves, had amazing self-worth, who knew how to love and nurture us so that we grew up believing who we were born to be.

The reality is there are not too many of us who were born to perfect loving parents who knew how to love us as they loved themselves. But our parents did the best that they could at the time, so please consider giving up blaming your parents for your life now as an adult.

As children and adolescents, we make sense of how our parents loved each other and as adults we either replicate what our parents did, do the opposite, or attempt different versions of what love is and what it is to be loving based on our experiences as a child. Few parents consciously teach their children what love is, but there is much unconscious learning by osmosis from our families.

If you grew up with parents that fought, or one person had more power over the other, you may believe that is what you need to do to be loved, or you may resist and do the opposite. Some of us for the strangest of reasons have thought we need to give ourselves up to be loved. What we don't realise, until we have suffered, is all the giving in the world does not necessarily mean that we will be loved in return.

Some of us don't know how to give love to ourselves. So we feel that to be loved, someone has to be endlessly filling us up with their love. If you are like this, you are still learning how to give love freely and how to receive love. If you have not learnt how to self-care consider the idea that you may be gaining your need for approval from another source. If you are not giving to yourself it is likely you have become a taker, even though you may think you are a giver. What you may have learnt in life was to give to others so that you can take from others to get love.

What do people take for love and approval?

Energy

Emotional support

Spiritual connection

Friends

Acts of service

Money

Respect.

Rather than learning how to give these things to yourself, you may have learnt to take from other people, becoming what I call a 'modern-day vampire'. Modern-day vampires feed off the goodwill, kindness and generosity of others. Does this resonate with you?

If it does you may currently be in a relationship with a 'taker' or you may have been in one and are now starting to realise what happened. This could be a boss, a partner or a friend.

Noticing your inner crew

Noticing what you think but don't say, say but don't think and say without words?

What happens when you have made a commitment to something and it isn't quite what you had imagined?

If you change your mind, it affects somebody else. They are relying on you. But in your heart of hearts, it isn't really what you want to be doing anymore.

What do you do?

What are your inner crew, those thoughts in your head telling you to do or not to do?

The myth of imagining solutions

Veronica contacted me whilst she was travelling with a friend, Judith. She had agreed to travel with her for two months to help set up art exhibitions. While there was no formal agreement, Veronica felt like leaving the journey early, but was in a dilemma, as she did not want to abandon her friend. On the other hand the trip was not quite what she expected.

She said to me,

> *"The trip is not quite working out how I expected. I thought I would have more time to myself and to write in peace. I wanted to speak up and let Judith know I wanted to leave the trip early. The thought went around and around inside my head. I did not say anything, as I kept thinking I could manage, but I squirmed inside, bit my lip, and racked my brain looking for solutions for my needs, without actually saying anything. I started to imagine that we would come to a town and someone would say to Judith that they would love to travel with her, and I could just slip away without making a fuss. Or maybe we would hear from her partner and he would want to come over and take over from me."*

How many of us dream or complain about solutions to our problems without actually doing anything about them?

The hidden reality

So there was Veronica, travelling around Asia with an artist. Veronica was going to write during the day, and then at night support Judith with her exhibitions. She planned to see some of the countries and have fun at the same time. Sounds idyllic, right? After the first week, she realised that finding time to write was proving a little difficult. The days were filled with morning rituals: getting up, walking and breakfast. She said that was great. Then the travelling, finding out where to go, more travelling, finding accommodation, the venue and the set-up for the exhibition. She would have about 1.5 hours to write on some days.

She said she did her best, but the time to write seemed to get shorter and shorter. Judith had suggested Veronica write, after the ticket sales had ended for each exhibition. Veronica confided to me,

> *"Have you ever tried writing anything and been interrupted a thousand times? My train of thought would be lost, my flow diverted into many different directions. I was feeling pulled apart. My energy began to dissipate. I stopped being so excited about our travelling."*

I replied,

> *"Veronica, you don't have to do anything in life that you don't want to do. What if you were ill? Would you keep on going? Delaying and avoiding do not work."*

Veronica had made a commitment to Judith for two months. She had three weeks to go. She thought every day would pass quickly, and soon her two months would be over, so she thought there was no use in saying anything now. She kept on rationalising that she was enjoying the journey and that she just wasn't getting to fulfil her need to write. She could write when she had completed the journey.

Even so, she still felt compelled to change something. She was planning to speak up one day when she returned from a walk, but something else unexpected happened. She found a gift on her bed. She had made a comment about a handmade felt bag in a shop and Veronica bought it for Judith to show her appreciation. Judith knew this was kind and thoughtful, and once again delayed being frank with her companion. She told me, how Veronica had told her she was an easy companion to travel with and she enjoyed her as a travelling companion.

Judith's mind went into a spin. She wondered,

> *"Is this a trick? Is she manipulative and I haven't realised that yet? Is it just like being with my ex-partner who would say, 'You can come with me if you want, but this is what I am doing. And if you choose to come and you like it, great! Or if you don't, lump it'?"*

So she restrained herself again and again.

Exforming what needs to be let out

But then as what often happens when we repress an emotion, a crack opened and she blurted out,

> *"Well, I wish your partner would jump on a plane and meet us at our next venue, so I could stop, write and be still!"*

Oops. Now she had to handle the reaction. Life changes in a split-second. Veronica said she immediately felt better. She didn't have the tension in her body of withholding her feelings and not speaking her truth. Her body felt free again.

Creating new boundaries

Veronica told me they both negotiated some time on their own, staying in different places overnight and then meeting up the next day. Veronica found out that many people who travel on tours stay in different places to have their own space. She realised if she had only spoken up earlier she could have made the trip much more pleasant for both herself and her companion.

'Trying' not to offend someone, or trying to look after someone else and not having our own needs met, just doesn't work. Veronica finished the trip and maintained her friendship. Speaking up for what we need rather than tolerating something that doesn't work is so much better in the long run.

> *Veronica realised it would have been better to:*
> *Speak her truth at the first sign of tension*
> *Create loving boundaries for each other before the trip*
> *Make adjustments to the way they travelled together as new information appeared.*

If Veronica had not said anything, she would have spent the whole trip repressing her need for space, talking about it around the edges and ending up parting ways with her friend, with bottled-up emotions. Unless she knew how to release those emotions they may have turned inwards, created inner stress and barriers in other relationships. She would have kept avoiding speaking up about her needs with others in life. She started to break a habit of avoiding speaking about her needs.

The good thing is, the more we practise to speak up about our needs, the stronger we get at being calm and creating loving boundaries of respect for what we need in life. The reality is, our learning goes on forever as each new situation, event, or person comes into our life, bringing a new challenge to deepen our sense of who we are and what we need to be fulfilled.

SENSES

Without our senses, it's like living like being a cardboard cut-out. Empty of the body—all mind—no body.
—Waldorf Steiner

Waldorf Steiner wrote about our 12 senses in the early 1920s. His educational methods guide children to develop their 12 senses throughout their school years. If you were lucky enough to go to a Steiner school, you would be enriched by the experience of activating your sensory knowing. However, most of us were not that fortunate and we became focused on the mind—all things rational and sanitised.

We were told messages such as:

Think about things

Where is the logic in that?

Be objective

Stop being so soft

Don't touch

Don't get dirty

Don't smell

Don't play

Don't cry

Don't laugh

Don't be angry

Don't trust yourself

Don't trust your senses.

The consequence of all of these messages is often a suppression of sensing, feeling, intuiting and being free to play, dance, sing, draw or just have freedom to express ourselves in our unique ways.

If we do break out and be free in some way, we may end up having to deal with being humiliated by those around us, who respond by telling us to be sensible, be an adult, or be professional. We restrain our inner yearning to express ourselves once again and become a limited version of who we are and our potential as human beings. We:

Deny our intuitive knowing

Ignore what our senses tell us

Limit our play and curiosity

Limit our inner freedom

Limit our creativity.

The consequences are stress and overwhelm from over-thinking, detachment from human connection, loneliness, alienation, and we seek out temporary comfort in external things that become addictions, like food, alcohol, screens, technology, or consumerism.

Perhaps some of the very things we need to do are...

Dancing wildly in the rain

Drawing doodles with pen and paper

Listening to poetry

Putting our hands on the earth

Laughing and crying

Smelling flowers

Walking with our feet on the grass

Sharing heartfelt stories with friends

Hugging

Walking a dog

Sleeping

We are in a catch 22. We want to feel happiness and connection, yet we cut ourselves off from our senses, which enable us to sense the aliveness that we seek. We cannot escape the urge, and there are many reasons.

Physical reasons

We are at a critical time when, globally, sleep deprivation is a problem, along with obesity, stress, and many other chronic ailments which can be alleviated if we learn to trust our senses and instincts for creating our well-being—our instincts:

To sleep instead of overriding our need for sleep

To walk and not sit in meetings all day

To stand and not sit behind screens all day

To move regularly

To eat what nourishes not what creates obesity

To drink water

To eat locally grown organic foods

To make arts and crafts

To dance and sing

To meditate and to draw.

Human connection reasons

Managers and employers create distance between customers and employees. The more distant and 'professional' the employee is, the more aloof, the more a barrier is created between people. This barrier makes it more difficult to engage and talk about the things that matter.

This has consequences for both the managers and the employees. The managers feel isolated and alone, blame the systems, look for scapegoats, and attempt to use more and more technology to solve problems that are inherently more to do with relationships than technology. Not knowing how to be humble and build relationships across the barriers of position in an organisation results in limiting the growth of all concerned. The employees feel intimidated, not heard, repressed or bullied. The employees respond with absenteeism, presenteeism, and leaving in droves to either find the elusive perfect organisation where they are free to contribute in respectful relationships or create their own business.

Hence, a major problem in organisations is the lack of engagement by employees and the result is an ever increasing shift to self-employment and entrepreneurship as more and more people want the freedom to work for themselves.

The yearning for inner freedom and interdependence is inherent for all human beings.

We have been transitioning towards deepening connection with our senses and the freedom for mutually respectful relationships over the last 150 years. In the early 1900s people used their physical attributes, not their brains or their emotions, at work. In the mid to late 1900s people used their mind but were required to leave their feelings at the gate. Then, from early in the 2000s, people were now required to bring their emotional intelligence to creating and resolving workplace and relationship issues.

Today, while not many organisations would use the term 'spiritual', there is more focus on energy in the workplace and community.

A sense of aliveness

We are often so disconnected from what makes us feel well, happy and content we become depressed or seek out addictions to 'make ourselves feel good' on a temporary basis. We feed ourselves with manufactured food full of salts and sugars and manufactured tastes to numb our tastebuds.

We have forgotten what it is like to feel full and overeat, resulting in obesity as one of our modern-day ailments.

We misconstrue our sense of needing water with hunger, so we eat when we need to drink.

We suffer stress because we do not sense the early warning triggers that our body sends us to ease tension and give ourselves what we need to be well.

We have lost the sense of our aliveness. As we move further into rational and technological thinking, we are taking life to the edge of our humanity.

We need to re-centre. To become grounded. To come home to our body, where we reside, while we are alive on this earth.

Scientists made the split between body, mind, and energy to study humans. This resulted in major breakthroughs, but we are greater than the sum of our parts. To sense and feel a connection between our thoughts, senses and physicality grounds us to ourselves and the world around us.

In a grounded state, we can feel our emotions, sense our energy and aliveness. We can learn to interpret messages through our senses that guide us to states of well-being.

We are so busy thinking that we often do not stop, pause and ask, "How am I thinking? Is my way limiting? How can I embrace other ways? Will other ways of thinking create better outcomes that are more ethical and respect me, others and nature?"

Even if we stop, pause and ask ourselves these questions and others, we have been trained to think objectively so well, it is hard to escape the objective virus that has been implanted. Therefore, we will tend to think about the questions with our same thinking and omit other kinds of knowing from our sensory and energetic capacities.

Our skin has intelligence. Our gut has intelligence. There is intelligence in the very rooms that we inhabit.

I have learnt to connect with my thoughts, my body senses, my physicality and energetic qualities of my being, and the being of others and my environment. It is the capacity to be both in my body with my thoughts and outside of them in parallel spaces that has given me both immense freedom and joy.

What is this kind of thinking, which is expansive? How can we illuminate the nature of our thinking? Not as an abstract, mental activity but as a felt, visceral, grounded process of living and being.

Are you thinking and connecting your thoughts to a multiple sense of yourself?

Your lived experience

Your senses

Your emotions

Your imagination

Your ethics

Your values

And to a sense of the people and the environment you are with?

The air

The energy

The visceral environment

The relationship with others

The sense of connectedness or alienation

Or are you thinking in your head, playing around with abstract ideas as if they live out there in the ether, and are not grounded in your lived experience? Are you thinking as if thoughts and ideas are rational, objective things that are more important than our lived experience, more important than the felt embodiment of our humanity and sense of being?

Are you ignoring your felt experience of a situation?

Why would I ask such a question?

What is the question the World asks of me?

The more time we spend on technology, the more it is as if we are living our world vicariously through 'the body' of technology (yet technology is not a living entity), out there, outside of ourselves, or inside our heads, in a world of ideas.

Humans and animals do have a natural capacity to leave their bodies to protect themselves. The more stress we have in the world, the more there is a natural survival mechanism of escaping our bodies to protect ourselves. We have a protective mechanism, so we do not feel pain and trauma. Most of us have forgotten to shake out the trauma and reconnect to our body when we are safe. We escape our body to protect ourselves from pain and do not shake out the tension. Before we know it, we live outside of our body most of the time. We are so accustomed to being in this state that we don't even know we are living in a world of ideas, not connected to an embodied sense of ourselves and others!

Why does it matter?

When your ideas are abstract and your thoughts are not connected to body, as a consequence you may feel:

Alienation from self

Disconnection

Aloneness

Stress

Limitations in feeling safe, content and fulfilled.

In our aloneness amidst a sea of relationships, we may experience consequences such as:

Relationship breakdowns

Tensions

Unethical choices

Cover-ups

White lies

Inhumane actions

Defensiveness.

Every time we discount our senses, our intuition, or our feelings and act as if our ideas and rational thought are outside of ourselves, we are destroying our humanity and limiting the creative intelligence that can arise from embodied thought.

Thinking from a rational disconnected perspective is more likely to create our relationships with others, workplaces and communities within a milieu of:

Fear

Intimidation

Bullying

Control

Pretence

Cover-up

Defensiveness.

We compromise our ethics when we are disconnected; we limit our creative intelligence and the emergence of new and better ways to live our lives and create our workplaces and communities.

We place limitations on ourselves and others that are more to do with protection and control, minimising emotion, coercing and manipulating others into agreeing that our way is right and another way is wrong.

What happens when instead we connect thinking to our body, our senses, our emotions and our lived experience?

The results for ourselves are:

Freedom

Expansion

Connection

Alignment.

For others:

Empathy

Engagement

Respect

Reciprocity

Collaboration

Creative expansion

New intelligence.

When we connect thought and language to our body and senses in a state of love and respect, we create the conditions for our intelligence to emerge in a safe and respectful environment—the unseen, unspoken space humans need to feel safe, to share, to be non-defensive, to trust, to take risks, and to allow new ideas and actions to emerge that have the potential to benefit our humanity.

Then we can connect to our inner body language.

INNER BODY LANGUAGE

When do we sense an inner body language?

In the briefest moment of a pause, we have the capacity to enrich our thinking from within our body, senses and energy. We can learn the language of this inner intelligence in much the same way as we learn to speak and to read words. Many of us read body language from another person. We observe someone's physical body and notice changes in posture, voice tone, movement and language as we communicate to help us understand each other. We do this both subconsciously as well as intentionally.

In the pause are spaces to listen in sense and notice

There is also an inner body language to guide us to a state of well-being. When we pause, we can turn to our senses, our noticing and intuitive capacities to become aware of what our inner body is guiding us to do, think and be for well-being. The purpose of inner body language is to restore our well-being, to access boundless energy and creativity and to surface unknown wisdom. In the pause, we can see, sense, notice, embody, play, and intuit meaning from our body language from the inside out.

The wisdom is in our innate sensory capacities. In accessing the rich information we have from our senses, it is like shifting from black and white television to digital technicolour. Our perception of ourselves and the world gains clarity, richness and depth, way beyond what we see when we are machine-like and rational. All the rational thinking in the world will not turn off our capacity to feel and sense.

Declaring I will not allow myself to feel and sense beauty, compassion, to be touched by a human heart does not mean I can turn off the essence of being human.

But we have pretended we can. In our workplaces and relationships, we have pretended we can turn off our emotional, sensory and energetic capacities and operate as if we are devoid of emotion.

The latest statistics on stress in the workplace and at home, on bullying at work, on disengagement at work, absenteeism and presenteeism are all indications that we cannot turn off the essence of our humanity. In attempting to disable our humanity, we contribute to the stress that has now in itself become a problem to face.

The early adopters of creating workplaces where people can be human, like Google, Amazon, Gravity Payments and GoldCorp, are thriving. People are wilfully sharing more of their creative energy and discretionary effort when given permission to be human at work.

The shift is happening. The more we turn towards our humanity, including being with our senses, our emotions, our energy and our stories:

The more we use descriptive, sensory language to share stories about ourselves.

The more we put our hands back into the soil, grow our food and bake our bread.

The more we re-engage with our whole body, mind and energy through walking, dancing, meditation, or yoga.

And the more we are creating the conditions for tapping into our creative intelligence.

The shift to amplify our sensory, imaginal and energetic body is happening in all kinds of ways.

Have you noticed the rise of these activities?

Adult colouring books

Adults participating in playgroups and InterPlay

Home-made products

Grow your own, organic, cook your own

Work from home, meetings in coffee shops, daily walks

Being in nature

Face to face

Walk and talk meetings

Stand-up meetings

Handmade arts and crafts

A plethora of bodywork, yoga, dances, massages

Art shows on television.

What is common to all of these simple activities is a pull back into being in our bodies in either the natural world or an imaginal world that we are creating through art, beauty, and craftsmanship. We are attracted to these activities by an unconscious pull—a pull back into our bodies and our instincts.

These simple activities are becoming commonplace and are drawing us back into what aids humans to thrive. Making, creating, playing, walking, breathing, relaxing, sensing in a state of curiosity, awe and wonder for the world around us. We are human beings, not human machines. While I love technology, and it gives us many benefits, we must remember it is one of our tools. We do not need to become the machine. A machine does not need light, fresh air, companionship, art, beauty, camaraderie, fresh food or exercise. Humans do.

As machines replace many more mechanical tasks, we have more opportunity for human work that cannot be done by a machine. Humans create relationships, art, beauty, laughter, family, community. Humans grow and cook food.

Many years ago there was a prediction that the four-day working week would come. It did not, and instead the opposite surfaced. People at work doing intellectual work with technology can now work 16-hour days and never turn off. This is not healthy for humans. Pretending we are machines that can work around the clock has created stress, tension, conflict, ill health, strained relationships, family conflict and much more.

The more we have moved away from our humanity, the more we have increased modern-day disease. Our problems are also our opportunities. Our problems tell us we are doing something wrong.

Could it be that our stress and depression is telling us we are doing something wrong?

It is stressful to 'live inside your head'

It is stressful to live in concrete jungles without green space and nature

It is stressful to work with a computer all day and night

It is stressful to communicate via technology all day without human connection

It is stressful to multi-task.

The biggest cities in the world, like Chicago, are laying earth over rooftops, and creating walkways, bike pathways, and gardens. Not only are cities too hot without earth and plants, concrete jungles come with drainage problems. People also need places to breathe fresh air, walk in green space, grow plants, enjoy natural sunlight and converse. That is being human.

I love science, but as I said earlier, do we have to wait for scientific research to tell us nature is good for us? If we listen to our bodies, our bodies tell us all the time what brings us to life and what slows us down. Our bodies know nature is good for us. Our bodies instinctively know walking is good for us. As they know breathing fresh air is good for us and going to bed at a reasonable hour for seven or more hours sleep is what we need to function well. To go to sleep in the dark and wake up with the light connects us to a natural rhythm of the universe, to life itself.

We are being called to return to a more natural state that is more in rhythm with life itself rather than the 'manufactured' one we thought we could impose upon ourselves throughout the manufacturing era.

The shift has begun, and it will only expand in new ways the more we lose our tolerance for amnesia and life draining products. The more we create our workplaces into places that sustain body, mind and spirit, the more fulfilled we will become and the more prosperous in people and life terms.

There is less depression and anxiety in workplaces that focus on helping people thrive. We are more creative with our colleagues in an environment conducive to trust, acceptance, and connection. The more we sense what is life-giving, the more we can speak about what works and what doesn't in ourselves, our relationships, our workplaces. From this position, the more we can make a stand for the truth from our politicians, the leaders of business, our educators, farmers and spiritual leaders.

As we come back to our senses, we can make choices that are good for our whole well-being. When we pause, shift from our thoughts to our senses, to our energy, to the energy of the room and the people we are with, we can make choices that are both good for others, our environment and ourselves.

When we pause too long and sit on the fence, going to and fro with thoughts not connected to what our body is sensing, we make ourselves unwell. Thoughts buzzing around endlessly without a physical connection are tiring and generate anxiety. We may become paralysed and do nothing to change what we wholeheartedly want to change. When we do not take actions towards ease and contentment, we stay stuck in a spiralling state of stress.

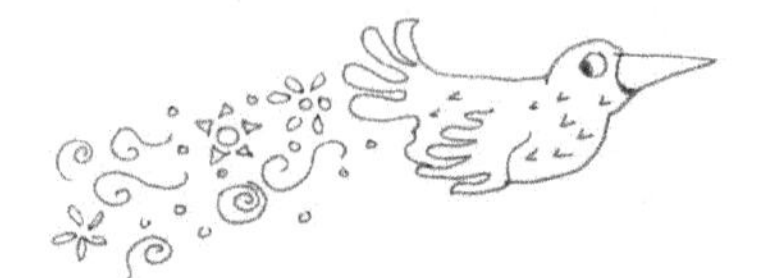

I learnt how over-thinking was paralysing when I stayed too long in a de facto relationship that exhausted me and eroded my self-worth. I kept 'thinking' I could do something different to change the way my ex-de facto treated me. I ignored how my body felt de-energised and how I felt my sense of self-worth eroding. If I had connected with my inner body intelligence and listened sooner rather than later, I could have alleviated much stress in my life. I could have chosen to be with people at work and in the community who respect each other and where there is no need to change myself or anyone else as mutual respect exists.

When we are disconnected from our sensory, emotional and spiritual body, we make choices from that disconnected place. We may lack compassion for ourselves, perhaps giving up our needs for others, or we may blindly be selfish and create our success at the expense of others. Neither of these ways is successful.

Have you ever had a sense of being grounded? Feeling as if you have come home into your body? Have you had a feeling of being out of the body? When you begin to notice the difference, you can consciously shift your state to what you sense is being centred. The more centred we are, the more we are connected to our whole self and our truth. From this centred place in our body, we can learn to trust ourselves.

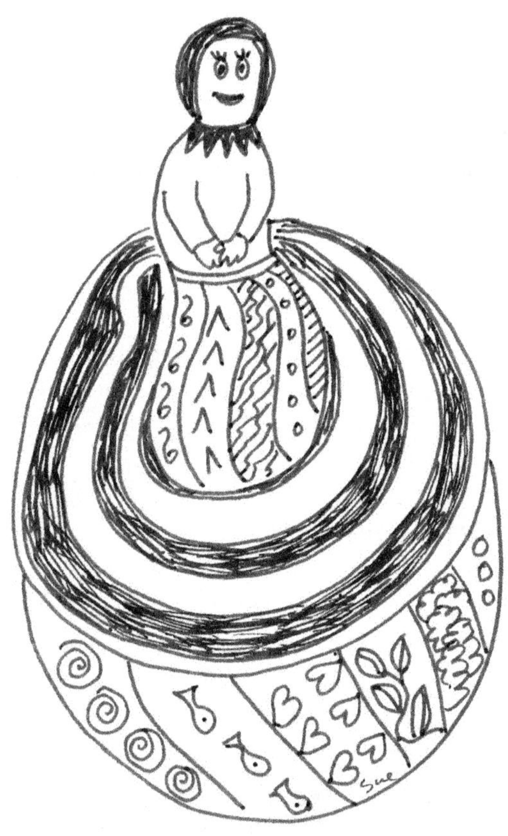

TRUST

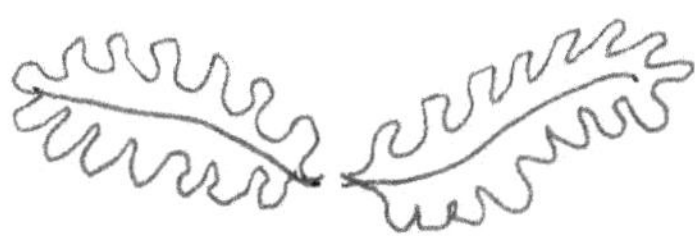

Trust is the glue of life. It's an essential
ingredient in effective communication.
—Stephen Covey

Learning how to trust our senses, which are as old as the human race and its predecessors, reconnects us with ancient wisdom carried in the roots of our DNA. We experience senses on the inside and the outside of our awareness. I sense these boundaries are fuzzy, so I have included my experience of an inside and outside awareness of our senses. For example, 'touch' is a physical experience through touching an object, and we can have the experience of being emotionally 'touched', which evokes a physical sense, warmth in the heart and visceral experience.

Inside life—a sense of well-being and aliveness

Inside movement—being aware of the inter-relationships of our body parts moving

Outside movement—sensing movement in our environment

Outside balance—an orientation of up, down, right and left

Inside balance—an orientation of feeling grounded or balanced between thinking, feeling and acting

Inside touched—being touched with human warmth and connection that stirs positive emotion

Outside touch—the physical experience of touching another object and also a sense of safety or danger

Outside taste—flavours which carry a sense of safety or danger

Outside smell—sensing odour carried in the air and warning of possible safety or danger

Outside sight—sensing images in the outside world

Inside sight—sensing thought as images and in our dreams

Outside warmth—our physical warmth and temperature in our environment

Outside speech—a sense of hearing our thoughts as words with a tone and pitch

Outside thought—a sense of thinking before verbalising thought into speech

Outside ego—a sense of 'I' as distinct from another.

Inside intuition—intuiting one's intelligence

Outside intuition—intuiting patterns of collective intelligence

Inside energy

Outside energy.

I added energy and intuition, although these are more a synthesis of our multiple senses. Energy could also be the sense of our aliveness. If we live with an awareness—either inside our head in the world of ideas, or outside ourselves in a virtual world—we miss the connection of what we are doing that is creating a sense of aliveness or lack of aliveness.

Even our digital and rational world seems to be pulling us towards our senses. The digital world was once black and white, now we have "touch" screens, video, audio, 3D. It is as if we can not ignore our senses. Our body knows better than we think. I imagine there is an unconscious collective pull to reconnect to our body and our instincts. A plethora of trends taking us back into connection with the body:

Emotional intelligence

Body intelligence

Body related therapies

Body and movement activities

Play and creativity

Colouring in

'Touch' screens

'Sensory' technology for cars

Written word either embellished or abandoned for images and video

The sleep revolution

Story telling.

Thinking and speaking with abstract theoretical words is the way most of us thought was credible. It was supposed to evoke a sense of professionalism and knowledge in a world that looked up to education, credentials, titles and positions. Speaking in abstract language and theoretical jargon some look and sound more intelligent than those who did not have this language. But today, most people have an education, can read, write and access information and they want to engage, connect and understand.

Today abstract and theoretical language is more associated with pretence and ego.

In response to alienation from abstract language there is a trend today towards storytelling. People are re-learning an ancient art of speaking using metaphors, imagery, and descriptive language. The new but old art of storytelling is generating connection and understanding where abstract language has failed.

Storytelling from the heart is the truth of someone's experience.

Authenticity gives us credibility today.

Authenticity builds relationships and connection.

Theoretical language can create distance and can disconnect us from our whole-bodied intelligence: emotional, sensory, imaginal and spiritual. We are overlooking the gold within our intelligence when we remain in a rational, abstract world. We lose sight of having a human conscience and become incongruent with our humanity. If we cut off our emotion and only talk in abstract, theoretical language, how humane and ethical are our choices?

Authenticity is an alignment between what we think, say, do and feel. When we are authentic, we are believed and trusted. When we are inauthentic, we are doubted and not believed.

Developing our capacities to notice, sense and gain access to our multiple intelligence through our senses is critical if we are to be more authentic.

When we develop our sense of trust in our intuitive capacities, we find simplicity in complexity.

It does not matter whether you are a scientist, an engineer or a retailer, we have all been impregnated with the rational virus so we seek answers outside ourselves from experts and research rather than from making sense of our own experience. Logic and rational thinking processes are relevant for specific purposes; i.e. construction, engineering, and technology. But when we come to work with people, inter-relationships, and systems, we need to access different ways of making sense of complexity.

William Bruce Cameron's words are relevant: "It would be nice if all of the data which sociologists require could be enumerated because then we could run them through IBM machines and draw charts as the economists do. However, not everything that can be counted counts, and not everything that counts can be counted."

FROM THINKING TO SENSING

A young woman came to me perplexed about whether to stay in her job or whether to start her own business. She said she could not see a way of staying in a relationship with her husband if she chose to start a new business.

We paused. I invited her to sense how her body felt about the three different choices that she was considering.

I asked her to express what she was thinking in three different scenarios,

1. Staying in her job and staying with her husband
2. Leaving her job and staying with her husband
3. Leaving her job and her husband and starting a new life.

She began sharing what she was feeling about whether to stay with her husband or not. I asked her to stop and pause. I asked her to connect with the words that she had just said about her husband in her body. I asked her to breathe. Tears came to her eyes. She began to speak of the love and loyalty of her husband. I asked her to stop again and sense her body after she had spoken. Tears began to well in her eyes again. She felt the presence of his love, his loyalty and his commitment to her whether she chose to leave the job or stay in the job. He had given her the freedom to choose. He was there for her, even if that meant them living apart for a while.

Through allowing her to sense a connection between her thoughts and her body, she leant into her body and her body released the feelings that she had contained. Her tension was released, or 'exformed', through the release of tears.

She had been stuck in the question: "How can I pursue my dream, which meant moving locations, and also stay with my husband?" She felt paralysed as she did not want to leave her husband, but she knew he could not transfer to a new location for nine years.

Once she made a connection with her body, she became present to his love and her love for him. While she was in the world of ideas and thoughts, she was disconnected from the sense of love within her and within their relationship. She could not sense the loyalty, the life, the well-being, the backing, the trust and the wish that he had for her to fulfil her dreams. He was giving her permission to pursue her dreams and saying he would come at a later date, but she could not be present to the experience of love and loyalty until she paused and felt it in her body.

At the moment when she paused, she sensed her physicality. She did not think when she paused. She connected to her energetic, emotional and sensory body experience of the love she had for her husband. We were talking on Skype from two different sides of the earth, and we could only hear each other, yet I felt the energy of love between them.

She realised she could stay in her relationship, which she had not realised before as she had not sensed the freedom and support from her husband. She could only see roadblocks and barriers that she was creating herself.

Now that the tension concerning leaving her husband no longer existed, she could concentrate on her primary question:

"What is my passion and what does that mean for the work that I choose?"

Her choice was easier when she had made the connection between mind, body, and energy. I asked her to imagine staying with her husband and sensing the freedom of pursuing a passion whether she stayed in her job or whether she chose to leave her job.

I asked her to walk into the physical experience of leaving her job. She immersed herself in an experience of tasting, touching, smelling, hearing, imagining, and feeling the experience of leaving her job and walking into another job. In essence, embodying her dream right now in the present moment.

It was likely she would have left her husband if she had continued doing what most people do, which is write lists or do a strengths, weaknesses, opportunities and threats analysis, as she created barriers in her head with abstract ideas. When she 'thought' about leaving her husband, her body showed her tension, anxiety, and a sense of jumping off a cliff without a safety net. When she learnt to apply all her senses, her body showed her ease, grace and freedom in making the choice to stay with her husband.

She had been reading her physical and energetic senses incorrectly. She 'thought' the choice to stay or leave was controlled by her husband. She realised she was free to choose and she was creating limitations and obstacles within her ideas.

Many people leave respectful relationships 'thinking' there is something wrong with the other person when it is something within ourselves. Others leave workplaces only to find themselves in a new situation with a manager or workmates with similar behaviours that triggered the emotions they wanted to leave behind. Of course, the opposite is true, where people stay in relationships or workplaces that are abusive, often thinking they are responsible for someone else's behaviour and can do something to change or control the other person.

Having the ability to stop and notice what we can control and what we cannot increases our chances of success. Our ability to sense a connection between thought and body creates the space for ease, grace and new understanding.

The Second Rite of Passage—Instincts, Noticing and Sensing in Daily Life

Getting in touch with your true self must be your first priority.
-Tom Hopkins

AN EVENT IN EVERYDAY LIFE

Life isn't about waiting for the storm to pass.
It's about learning to dance in the rain.
-Vivian Greene

Roland

I was coaching a client, Roland, who was working with a group of people in extremely challenging conditions. He had facilitated a session that had gone very well. During the session, Roland was aware of some differences in approach by the two leaders. In a private conversation, the leaders had shared some stories as to how they resolved those differences. Roland shared some of these stories with his work team to help them understand some ways to resolve differences.

While this was extremely effective for the group, he had not sought permission from the leaders to share these stories as an example, as it had only occurred to him in the present moment. One leader, Bob, could see how useful sharing the example was, while the other leader, John, took offence. John did not speak to Roland about the feelings that arose nor did he reflect and take responsibility for understanding his reaction. The 'offence' lay brewing and turned into anger and judgement against Roland.

John finally called in Roland. "Ronald, last week every time I saw you speaking with Bob I thought the two of you were both colluding against me. I think I am probably making up this story but I do not like the two of you working together. You are making lots of suggestions for the ways we could do things and I don't want you to. I am the leader and I will make the decisions with my co-leader, Bob. If I want your suggestions I will ask for them."

John asked Roland if there was anything he wanted to say in response.

Roland said, "Well, I am glad you said you are probably making up this story of Bob and me colluding against you. As you know, Bob and I are friends and we have not worked with each other for a long time, and we have lots to catch up on. Of course we are not colluding against you. As for the suggestions, I do not expect you to act on them; I am merely offering ideas."

"That is all," John said, and Roland was dismissed.

Roland told me he had wanted to say, "I think you are projecting your own issues about being threatened by others' success on to me."

However, he did not speak his thoughts. He felt intimidated. John had requested Roland not to speak up, so he did not want to rock the boat any further. He told me they had two more weeks to work together and he said it was best to smooth things over.

Ronald thought he could let his feelings go even though John was showing behaviour towards him that was controlling, judgemental, authoritarian and disrespectful. Roland continued to do what was expected in his role, but as the days passed there were many times when the group was talking about a project and he felt inhibited to speak. He was controlling himself to meet John's demands. He said he could feel his anger rising. John now seemed to think he could continue to control Ronald, to bully, dominate and be autocratic with the group and towards Ronald. Roland said he felt pushed and pulled, and that he could not do anything right.

Roland's body started to seethe with emotions. He wondered whether he needed to speak up or whether to let it go. I coached him to listen to his feelings. He was sad and angry from being controlled, dominated, judged inaccurately, blamed for something he did not do and then punished. As he felt his energy for contributing diminishing, he started to feel small. I asked him what he needed to do for himself to restore his authentic self. He said he needed to let John know the consequences of his behaviour towards him. I coached Ronald how to talk to John and share the effect his words and directives had on him without blaming him.

Ronald initiated a conversation with John. "John, I felt crushed the other day when you spoke to me. I felt punished. I felt like I had to take responsibility for the assumptions and feelings that arose in you when I was facilitating a very successful session. This does not work for me. I have been controlling myself since you told me not to contribute. I am giving you back responsibility for your feelings, thoughts and assumptions."

To Roland's surprise, John apologised. He said, "Yes, I thought after our conversation that I was blaming you, but I did not realise this would impact you. I guess I needed to let you know what insight I had gained. Thanks for letting me know."

Roland was at peace with himself again. He had given himself a voice. He had been respected and he had not blamed John. Roland realised that if he had spoken his truth in the first place rather than protecting himself and Bob, he would not have spent days being uncomfortable. However, he also acknowledged himself for having the courage to take responsibility for his feelings and to hand back the responsibility for someone else's assumptions to them.

Roland had learnt to listen to the call of anger.

ANGER IN EVERYDAY LIFE

There is always a great lesson to learn. In Roland's story, he was at first content. Then he had an experience that he found disrespectful yet he chose to be silent. His body could not be silent. His energy, behaviour and sense of self changed until, without expecting, his body expelled his agitation. He then learnt to speak up when disrespected, sense what messages his body was sharing, and learn to shift back to neutral, content states.

At times we can release our anger and claim respectful boundaries without speaking up to the person concerned about a past event. It is an acute sensitivity to be aware of when it is best to discuss the situation openly with the person or when we can alter the relationship through changing ourselves, without open conversation.

While I have used anger and disrespect as examples for this explanation, we can apply the principles of learning an inner language from our body, senses and intuitive capacities to situations where we feel frustrated, fearful, disappointed, or any other emotion that expresses itself in your body. No matter what the source of an irritation, or our response, we can find new ways to sense the meaning that our body is making and how to restore our well-being.

Heeding the early signs

Some of us were taught to suppress our feelings and others to let them out, but few of us have learnt to understand that all of our feelings are a language. We can learn to understand our feelings and senses just as we have learnt to understand words.

Anger is an emotion that screams out in our bodies when we are allowing ourselves to be disrespected, or there is injustice in the world. When anger appears, often we have been ignoring an early warning, or tolerating something that is not serving us.

If we can begin to notice the first signs of any irritation, we can give ourselves what we need to heal the source of our discontent quickly. Healing the source enables us to be more of who we are born to be: joyful, happy and at peace. The more we ignore, cover up and suppress an emotion, the more it grows. The more it grows, the more we are likely to hurt ourselves and others.

Not speaking up for your true self, or allowing yourself to be disrespected, judged, or controlled, can lead to frustration, which can grow into resentment and, ultimately, anger. When these emotions are repressed, they lead to a dulling of our spirit, or are expressed in an outrage of vindictive, mean words and actions. Neither of these ways are loving to ourselves or others.

If we can listen to the first sign of discontent, we then have the choice to empower ourselves and take responsibility for ourselves, take loving actions towards our self, and heal the discontent from disrespect or injustice in the world. Discontent transforms when we take loving actions towards ourselves. We can be free to express our true authentic loving nature when we acknowledge those parts that arise that we do not like.

Let's take a look at your experiences with anger.

What do you do when you are angry, frustrated or agitated? Ignore the first sign at your peril! Do you explode, deny being upset or shut down and withdraw? Do you say to yourself and others, "I never get angry, frustrated or annoyed", while seething under your skin?

When was the last time that you were angry? What boundary did you let someone step over? How did you restore your safety and respect?

Anger has a purpose. What was the purpose of your anger?

Responding to the early signs

Every emotion has a purpose. The sensory experience we call anger has served us well to make us aware of a possible threat to our well-being. If we acknowledge that usefulness, listen well, respond skilfully and be resilient, we can come back to our state of love. It is what we do with it and how we act that will make a difference to living well.

If we do not understand anger, hold onto it, repress it or let it take us over, the anger becomes misdirected. The anger calls out to us to give ourselves what we need to regain respect, or whatever it is that we lost, in some original event. If we do not listen, it will call out by either 'blowing up' when reminded of the event or by controlling us to live our lives in a restrained expression of who we really are. Repressed anger can control our lives unconsciously, as it did with Roland, and will appear long after the original event to trouble you until you give yourself what you need to free the anger from the cellular memory in your body.

To successfully process and release anger, we need awareness and skill to listen, access the message from the anger, act with purpose to restore our respect and come back to our loving self.

In this section, I am not talking about the rage or anger of suicide bombers, warmongers, or people who have so much anger they want to kill anyone who does not have their beliefs. That would take this book to another level of complexity. Here I am talking about anger that occurs in our personal lives.

MANY TRUTHS

I invite you to determine what your truth is about anger. First, I am going to share two truths that I have experienced about anger. I have experienced what I call 'rightful' anger, which leads to responsible action and protection of safety, respect and/or justice. I have also experienced anger and actions as a result of repressed anger, which have led to adverse consequences for myself and others. My body is now empty of residual anger from past events, so they do not control my life anymore. I now know when anger surfaces, it is a warning that I may be disrespecting myself, I may be allowing someone else to cross a boundary of disrespect, or I may be fired up to act for others about injustice in the world. If I am angry, I have ways to be with it, to listen to the message, to release the energy respectfully and come back to my loving self. I respect anger if it surfaces and I act in ways that give it release.

Let's look at one situation and three different responses to the anger that surfaces by reacting to the same event. It is my intention to help you uncover the skills you may need to learn and practice to know the purpose of anger and take responsible action to create your safety and then come back to a loving, content state of being.

Three versions of the one event

Imagine you have a child and you are shopping. You turn away from your child to buy something at a roadside news stand, and when you look back you see someone offering a lollipop to your child and inviting them to get in the car with them.

Scenario 1: the purpose of anger and a skilful response

Your body swells into anger to protect your loved one and to stop a possible injustice. Questions race through your mind as you try to assess the situation. "What is happening? This is wrong! Who are you? What are you doing?" You run towards your child and call out, "STOP! Leave my child alone! Come back here, Susie!"

Your anger has propelled you into swift action to stop what is likely to be wrongful action and protect your child.

The car drives away and you sweep your child into your arms, your shoulders drop, you breathe deep, you may cry tears as you release the anger. You have taken skilful action to protect your child. You connect with the deep love you have for your child, you hug them and give them love. As you centre yourself and come back to a calm state, you say, "Some people are not safe. They may want to harm children. Never get into a car with someone you do not know."

Your child is safe.

Now you respond to the bigger picture, the safety of other children. You get on the phone immediately, call the police and tell them the colour of the car, the plate number, and which direction it was heading.

You are propelled into responsible action—to protect your child and to protect other children and the community.

The anger fades, as it has served its purpose.

Scenario 2: reacting, holding on to anger and blowing up

Your body swells into anger to protect your loved one and to stop a possible injustice. Questions race through your mind as you try to assess the situation. "What is happening? This is wrong! Who are you? What are you doing?" You run towards your child and call out, "STOP! Leave my child alone! Come back here, Susie!"

You yank your child away from the car and rage at the person who is driving away. You end up being in such an angry state, your child is now frightened of you. You hang on to the anger and project your anger onto the child, "What did you do that for, you stupid child! Never do that again!"

You blame the perpetrator and you blame the child.

The child becomes confused, wondering exactly what she did wrong. Children do not know that your anger is over the top because of your love for them and your reaction to the possibility of them being harmed. You forgot to tell them that you love them and are happy they are safe, as you are so angry. You do not know how to release the anger to come back to a loving state.

You may stay angry with the person who could have harmed your child for a long time. They are not present, so you cannot direct your anger at them, and you feel helpless at not being able to stop this person, seducing children into their car. You project your anger onto other people around you when they suggest that you calm down, that the event is over. "What would you know?" you yell at them.

You do not connect with your sadness and helplessness underneath the anger. You forget that your anger is about protection and the love for your child. You begin to overprotect your child, restricting your child's freedom and ability to learn responsibility and safety for themselves.

Your child gets angry with you for constraining their freedom and being unfairly angry with them. This snowballs over time into sore points in your

parent-child relationship. You wonder why you and your daughter rub each other the wrong way and imagine all sorts of reasons over time. You attempt different things to resolve your antagonism.

The original event gets buried deep but it is still boiling inside under a lid in both yourself and your daughter waiting for a time to be released and healed.

It may be released over time as one or both of you 'get in touch' deeply with your body, your sensory experience and your emotions. At some later time in life, you may say, "Remember when....? I am sorry I reacted that way, I was so confused and hurt at the possibility of you being hurt that I became over-protective. Let us re-negotiate some boundaries so that we do not fight against each other and you learn how to be safe and have freedom within limits as you grow up."

Or perhaps neither of you ever gain access to releasing the emotion that was stored in your body after that event and your daughter talks about you like this: "Mum/Dad is so controlling. It was such a fight growing up to have any freedom." You and your daughter have a communication breakdown, and while you both do deeply love each other, there is a brick wall that neither of you know how to remove. You accept and tolerate the status quo as you do not have the skills to connect with your body, to release what has been trapped, to explore the beliefs that you took on at that time, i.e. "My daughter does not know how to protect herself. I have to be by her side until she is an adult. I have to protect my child or else she will be harmed. I cannot give my daughter her freedom. She will never be safe without me."

Your daughter unconsciously made up beliefs, too. Perhaps she made up a belief that she is not competent enough to create her own safety and she either becomes small and intimidated by others and is fearful in life, or rebels and takes risks that may cause her harm.

Scenario 3: reacting, repressing anger and being paralysed

Your body swells into anger to protect your loved one and to stop a possible injustice. Questions race through your mind as you try to assess the situation. "What is happening? This is wrong! Who are you? What are you doing?" You try to run towards your child and try to call out, "STOP! Leave my child alone! Come back here, Susie!"

But you are controlled and restrained. You go to speak and no voice comes out. You are paralysed. You feel helpless and you do not act at all.

Your daughter turns around catches your eye, and the offending person looks at you, quickly closes the car door and drives off. Your daughter walks over to you, but you cannot express the anger, the fear, the sadness, the possible loss. You are paralysed with grief and are now angry with yourself at not being able to help your child, at not being able to call out, at becoming paralysed, at not being able to throw your arms around your child, even though deep down you would love to. Your anger becomes repressed and you control your emotions, not allowing yourself to express love, anger, fear, grief or sadness. You abandon yourself and become a victim, not being able to take responsible action to come back to your loving self.

Your daughter is confused. As a child, she makes up an unconscious belief that you have abandoned her. Even though you are there, she does not feel your love. She has an emptiness that she may carry with her for life and not be able to give herself the love that she needs or receive love from others. Or she takes responsibility as a young adult to become aware and learn emotional skills and she connects with her emptiness. She gives herself the love that she needed from you at the time, and she finally frees herself from feeling abandoned and gives up blaming you for her emptiness.

Or back on that fateful shopping day, it could have been worse. You watch your child getting in the car and the car drives away. You are frozen on the spot, bewildered, and you cannot imagine what has happened. When you talk to the police later, you cannot even tell them the colour of the car as you are so upset and confused. It is as if you have left your body and cannot get back in. You are displaced. You feel vacant.

You blame yourself.

The police and your community judge you for being an irresponsible parent and you wither away inside, in grief and suffering, in self-flagellation. You become depressed. You cannot leave the house. The worst case scenario—you become suicidal.

You are stuck, paralysed, and you become a victim as you see no way to take responsible action and find a way out.

Three pivotal events in our life

There are many more ways the event could have panned out, and many different ways we could have responded. Looking just at the three described, the difference between the responses is skills and attitude. There were six key elements to the response in scenario 1 that led to the best outcome. These are:

1. Being present in the moment

2. Being able to respond swiftly in the moment

3. Being resilient enough that when back in a safe situation the anger energy has been appropriately dissipated and we can come back to our loving state

4. Being able to take responsibility for our awareness, our feelings and our actions

5. Being present to all of our physical sensory body and our emotions

6. Being willing to learn, be open and vulnerable.

We all have pivotal events in our life. In those pivotal events, we create meaning about ourselves, others and life that stays with us. When that meaning is unconscious, it is the fuel that ignites the ways we choose to act even if those ways sabotage us. When we are curious, playful and open up to surfacing the beliefs we have created, being present to our physical sensory body and our emotions, we can uncover and release what does not serve us. We can stop sabotaging ourselves and we can wisely choose what is the best for us at the time.

If we allow the beliefs to remain unconscious, they become a pattern of a way of being. We did the best that we could at the time, and if we recognise this, we can then learn something better later in life, rather than blame ourselves for the way we acted at some other time.

The skills and attitudes that sabotage us:

1. Being someone who blames yourself

2. Being focused on the past and not living in the present

3. Being closed and avoiding feelings

4. Being averse to collaborating and making choices that affect others on your own

5. Being averse to taking responsibility to learn and find ways of resolving tensions and challenges

6. Being controlling of your thoughts, feelings and energy and limiting the expression of yourself

7. Being controlling of others to create your own security and self-worth

As an adult, we have the ability to choose to reflect, become aware and become skilful at coming back to our true loving selves with the ability to be resilient and respond powerfully to life events. Until we learn from the beliefs we made up at the time, they have the capacity to control us.

Learning from animals

Think back to the paragraph in section 1 about prey animals and their reactions to danger and safety. A grass-eating animal has predators and needs to be sensing danger all the time. In the wild, a grass-eating animal is constantly grazing. It appears to be relaxed and content until it senses something in its environment. Its skin quivers, it may shake its tail, look up, stop grazing, prick up its ears, activate its sense of smell.

When it senses there is no more danger, it stops, it looks around, and it shakes off the tension from the flight and then goes back to grazing.

If it senses danger, it will flee, or if the attacker is close, the prey animal will either defend or pretend to be paralysed—roll up into a ball as if it is dead and putting off its attacker. Many animals fake death to defend themselves from predators. These animals shake out their paralysis when they sense they are back in safety.

When an animal defends itself, there is a moment when the animal knows it is captive and is going to be its predator's dinner. Scientists believe that the animal changes its state of being into a paralytic state to numb the pain of imminent death.

Wild animals live in constant threat of predators. If they held on to danger like humans hang on to emotions, their instincts would be clouded and they probably would not be able to function in the wild, just as human beings are limiting their functioning by 'hanging on' to emotions after events. A grass-eating animal's survival would be threatened if it never felt safe enough to graze.

What can we learn from the behaviour of wild animals in our civilised society?

Civilised society

Today I imagine that the human race has become so civilised, we have forgotten that we do have basic animal instincts, and in my view we ignore these primal senses at our peril.

While many people talk about us not needing to defend ourselves from 'woolly mammoths' as in Neolithic times, there are still many things to protect and defend today. For example:

Injustice

Disrespect

Violation of human rights

Psychological, emotional, spiritual, financial and physical abuse.

There are many actions and events from others in our lives that trigger an emotional response that may cause distress. If we do not resolve a situation our feelings may escalate into anger. How can we learn the skills to act with purpose, to make sense of our responses when they are small, and bring ourselves back into a content state?

In the next section, I share five different methods for you to explore. The application of each one will depend on how long you have been exposed to an injustice or been disturbed by an event.

What are you angry or irritated about?

There are as many things that you could be feel negative about as there are people in the world, but some of the common ones are:

Injustice from a parent

Injustice from a teacher

Being bullied at school or at work

Feeling responsible for something as a child and not having the skill to do what you wanted to do, so projecting your anger onto a parent

Feeling worthless

Having something of personal value taken away from you

Being asked to do something that compromise your values and doing it.

Anger in the past

If you have not been able to take just action and be resilient in the past to release anger and resolve an injustice, it is likely that this anger is stored in your body in your cellular memory. You may get triggered by anything that reminds you of the event; it could be the way someone speaks, what you hear, a room, a physical resemblance to someone, a tone of voice, a scent or an object. Whatever reminds you of the event triggers the memory, and the emotions arise even though the event is in the past. You may then project your anger onto the person or the event in the present, even if they had nothing to do with the initial event.

Anger in the present

When you learn to sense your anger arising as someone is about to do something that is disrespectful, you can learn to immediately create a respectful, loving boundary for yourself. When you stop a violation before it happens, you will not have residual anger in your body to release at a later date.

There have been few people teaching us how to understand our emotional states and to be resilient at coming back to love after we have been triggered emotionally by an event or a person.

Anger propels us to take action. How we take that action is up to how responsible and skilled we are at being present with our emotions, listening to our body/spirit and choosing to take 'right' action for the benefit of ourselves and others.

According to legend, a stone monument in a field in Wales marks the resting place of 'Gelert', the faithful hound of the medieval Welsh Prince Llewelyn the Great. The story, as written on the tombstone, reads:

> *In the 13th century Llewelyn, Prince of North Wales, had a palace at Beddgelert. One day he went hunting without Gelert, "The Faithful Hound", who was unaccountably absent.*
>
> *On Llewelyn's return the truant, stained and smeared with blood, joyfully sprang to meet his master. The prince alarmed hastened to find his son, and saw the infant's cot empty, the bedclothes and floor covered with blood.*
>
> *The frantic father plunged his sword into the hound's side, thinking it had killed his heir. The dog's dying yell was answered by a child's cry.*
>
> *Llewelyn searched and discovered his boy unharmed, but nearby lay the body of a mighty wolf which Gelert had slain.*
>
> *The prince filled with remorse is said never to have smiled again. He buried Gelert here.*

We do not have to be like Llewelyn, Prince of North Wales, and react with anger and later regret what we did. We can learn emotional resilience to breathe and respond wisely when we connect with our body wisdom and become highly skilled.

PRINCIPLES OF THE METHODS

Not an attack on someone else

The person who triggered the original resentment, irritation, injustice or anger may be alive, may be passed on, or may not be a part of your life anymore. You do not need their presence to do these processes, and in fact it is better not to have them present. It is best to not direct your repressed or unresolved anger at another person; you are more likely to stir up resistance and another fight if you want to 'get back at them' while you are releasing your unresolved anger.

Responsibility

These methods expect that you are taking responsibility for your emotional feelings and beliefs and you have an intention to learn and create a place of freedom and peace within you.

Curiosity

If you are curious and open when you play with these methods you may be surprised at what you find out. You may discover something new; therefore, having a curious attitude to exploring what shifts your anger and what doesn't is likely to lead the shift that you desire.

METHOD 1: A THREE-STEP PROCESS

I learnt method 1 from Dr Margaret Paul. [20] These steps were very beneficial to me when I needed to release my suppressed anger, when I did not speak up and felt powerless when I was violated.

There are three steps to the process. Do all three steps at the same time. Read through the exercise first, then organise a time to do the exercise.

STEP 1: Who are you angry with?

Choose a person or an event that is the source of your unresolved anger.

Give yourself permission to release the anger about this event and this person. If you are a person who is very expressive, give yourself permission to yell and use your whole body and your arms to express your anger.

Choose a safe place where you can yell and no one will hear you. Your lounge room, the shower, a park, the beach, the mountains—choose somewhere private.

Take a pillow or a soft cushion, or if you are outside you can use a wooden spoon, rocks or sticks.

Standing is preferable to make sure you have the freedom to move your arms and your legs. If in a room, you may kneel on your bed or on the floor and give yourself the freedom to beat your pillow.

Imagine the cushion is the person you are angry with and you are going to tell them all the things that have been rattling around in your head for a long time.

Take your cushion, throw it on the floor, pummel your hands into it, beat it and at the same time yell as if it is the person who has caused an injustice and tell them all the things that you are so angry about. If you are outside, hit your stick or rocks against the ground or another safe surface.

Really do it! Allow yourself to be angry. Let the anger come to the surface and beat it out. Express all the anger through words and actions to the cushion, tree, rock or water.

Stomp your feet, pace the room, yell and beat the pillow or throw it on the floor. It is really important to move—it releases pent-up emotions.

20 www.innerbonding.com

You may choose to do this on your own, but if you do want someone present, let them know you want them as a witness and explain their role. A witness does not judge, criticise, interfere or interrupt. A witness observes with love and acceptance. When you have finished you may invite them to share what they witnessed. Let them know you are not asking for their solutions or their advice. If you are concerned a witness will judge and advise you, do not ask anyone to be present.

Do you feel resistant about doing this? This is a great opportunity to explore your resistance. Resistance is a form of control. Unresolved anger will repress you in many ways. If this exercise does not work for you, there are many others.

We can draw, journal, run or talk the emotion out of our body. We can talk to our resistance and give ourselves permission to do something that releases our anger. Explore what it would be like to give up control and have the freedom to express this anger out of your body safely.

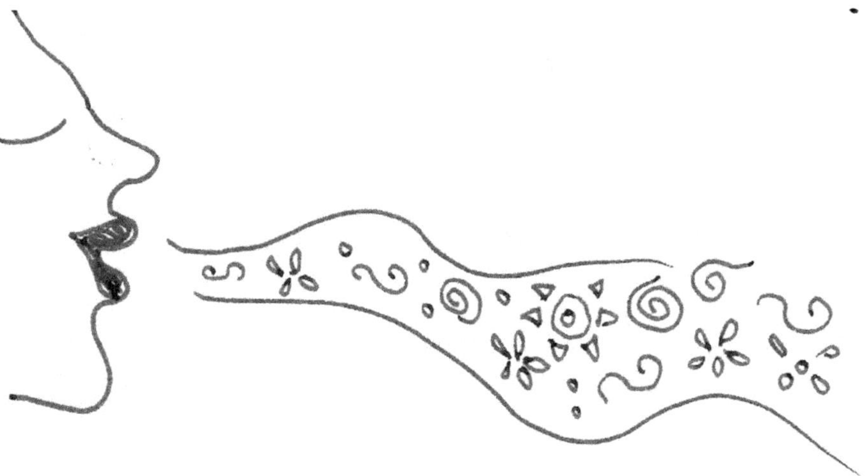

If you have taken yourself to a safe place and no one is there, you do not have to be embarrassed. As long as no one is there, you will not hurt anyone. There is no need to fear that the anger will overwhelm you—you are letting it rise so it can flow out of your body.

When you have had enough and you are exhausted from beating the pillow, or exhausted from yelling and there are no more words left to say, stop and take a breath.

Yes, breathe. Notice your breath.

When we are stressed or anxious, we have a natural reaction to shorten and tighten our breathing. We breathe into our upper body rather than deep into our belly. Short tight breaths do not give our cells the oxygen they need, and if we keep on taking short breaths, we will become more and more anxious and stressed. Just noticing your breathing and taking deeper, slower breaths can have a significant effect on your energy levels.

This is just the first step. Read on for Step 2 and Step 3 before you commence the exercise. If you want to write notes in a diary or journal, do so at the end of the exercise.

Step 2: Who else are you angry with?

Do a quick body scan and notice what other memory you have in your body of an event where someone was unjust and you had no power to stop the injustice.

Do the complete exercise as written in Step 1 again. This time direct your anger to the second person. Remember the person must not be present. You are saying what you would love to say to the air, the wind, the pillow or the dog.

Breathe. Move on to Step 3.

Step 3: What are you angry with yourself about?

It is likely that if you have unresolved anger, you are also angry with yourself. This is anger because you could not create safety for yourself or for someone else, anger that you tolerated abuse or anger that you let yourself be seduced, defrauded, manipulated etc.

Now do the whole exercise as outlined in Step 1 and direct all the anger that you have for yourself.

For example: Why didn't I do that? I am a stupid idiot! What made me allow X to do that to me? How could I have been walked over? Why didn't I stand up for myself?

Say all the things to yourself that you are angry that you did or did not do.

When you are exhausted and there are no more words and no more energy left, stop.

Surrender. Be gentle and kind to yourself now. Give yourself love and acceptance. Be at peace with yourself. If you feel like crying, cry. If you feel like sleeping, sleep. If you feel like rocking yourself like a baby, rock yourself like a baby.

Be in touch with what you need and give yourself that. Be the loving adult to yourself that you would have loved to have in your life.

If you feel like writing or drawing in a diary or a journal, do that after you have spent some time with yourself. Writing can take you out of your body and you need to stay present to what your body/spirit needs from you right now. Some ideas for you to explore in journaling are below.

Journal

What I know now about my anger with person X.

What I know now about my anger with person Y.

What I know now about my anger with myself.

METHOD 2: EXFORM—MOVE TALK MOVE TALK MOVE TALK

Allocate some time to yourself.

Find a safe place, i.e. your lounge room.

You may want to do this on your own, or if you choose to have someone with you, follow the witness principles: let them know you want them as a witness and explain their role. A witness does not judge, criticise, interfere or interrupt. A witness observes with love and acceptance. When you have finished, you may invite them to share what they witnessed. Let them know you are not asking for their solutions or their advice. If you are concerned a witness will judge do not ask them to be present.

Free-form movement

If you are reading this book, you will know I believe our bodies are talking to us, only we have forgotten how to listen. So much of our time is spent controlling our body movements, what we say and what we do, that we inhibit our body, our voice, our soul to speak through our body and voice.

When we give ourselves permission to be free and let our bodies and voice do the talking, new insights come to light that cannot be expressed when we are controlling what we want to say. In the exercise, 'Noticing Your Energy' in the 3rd section of this book, practise allowing your body to choose where it feels like walking down a street, noticing what your body is attracted to and what repels your body.

In this exercise, play with allowing your body to express itself freely. Do not think about how you will move or what story you will tell. Find a safe space to move around in, and move as long as you feel like moving.

When your voice feels a need to express something from the movements you are making allow yourself to speak. When you speak, you may speak in poetry, you may babble (sounds without words), or you may not be able to say the words that you want to so allow yourself to speak in made-up language. This is to free your voice and give yourself permission to speak from your heart and soul, saying what you really feel about the situation that is concerning you.

You can do this exercise two ways.

1. Follow the structure in method 1, only this time move and talk, move and talk, move and talk.

Each time you may choose to focus on three different events (as before, one main event that concerns you, a second event or person that concerns you, and your concern with yourself) or on one event only.

Any time you feel like you have some residual feeling in your body from an event or a person where you have not been able to restore justice, do something to return to peace; dance, write, draw, or talk to exform the emotion out of your body, free yourself from your anger, frustration or resentment and come back to peace with yourself.

A note on body play

Often we become restricted with the way we move our bodies. If you begin to give your body the opportunity to express itself with movement, you may be surprised by what your body knows before you have words and thoughts.

If you are used to dancing or moving a certain way, give yourself permission to move any way your body wants. If you feel restrained, start with your hand. Allow your hand and your arm to move and dance. When you feel a sense of freedom, let your other hand and arm join the movement and gradually extend this to the rest of your body.

Four ways to explore our body moving

Stillness and shape

Some people are more inclined to stillness. They may meditate, do yoga or Tai chi. You may wish to move slowly, like a tree that moves in the wind, return to stillness, move again as the wind picks up, and return to stillness. If you tend to move slowly and are usually quite still, make sure you practise and experiment with other body movements.

Hanging

Some people hang around. Do you ever let yourself hang? Or are you always tight like a spring? Practice what it would be like if you let your body hang. If you tend to 'hang', practise and experiment with other body movements.

Swinging

Some people are swingers. You can see it in their step and the way they swing their arms when they walk. Some people dance with a swing. Are you mainly a swinger? If you do not do much swinging, experiment with swinging, swing your legs one at a time, swing your arms one at a time. What is it like to walk with a swing, dance with a swing? What does that feel like in your body? If you are a swinger make sure you practise and experiment with other body movements.

Thrusting

If you are action-orientated, you may have a preference for thrusting. You may move in short, sharp, jerky movements like the karate kid. You may generally be a bold person. If you tend to move more with a 'thrust' make sure you practise and experiment with other body movements.

If you do not usually use bold movements, experiment with being bold. What does it feel like to be bold, to move sharply, confidently, courageously and protectively?

Music

You may wish to put on music to free your body to move. Music that does not have lyrics is the best. Remember, music affects your movement. At times move with the music and at other times move against the music.

Playfully, move and talk and move and talk and move and talk.

Give your body permission to move freely for as long as it wants, or at least a minute. When you feel your voice wanting to express your thoughts and your feelings allow yourself to speak. You may stop to speak about the feeling you are exploring, or you may want to keep moving. When that story or that voice has finished what it needs to say, move again. Keep giving your body the freedom to move. Give your voice freedom to express its even allow yourself to take on different character voices.

Journal

After doing a movement exercise, what do you know now about yourself and the feeling you are exploring?

What did your body and voice reveal when you gave them the freedom to move and speak without control?

METHOD 3: EXFORM WITH A JOURNAL

The purpose of this exercise is to exform the story of the event or the person who is triggering something that takes you away from being at ease with yourself.

Take a journal. Give yourself permission to write freely. Write whatever comes into your mind. It can be words, expressions, sentences, or it can be jumbled-up words or poetry.

This is called stream of consciousness writing. You do not have to worry about grammar, punctuation or spelling.

Write for at least 10 minutes.

Do this at least three times over three days, or for as long as you need to until you are spent. Do it until when you read the story back there is no more trigger. There is no anger. You are neutral.

When that occurs, then take another piece of paper or journal.

Now write a stream of consciousness about everything that comes to mind about how you are going to self-care and respect yourself and your loved ones in the future.

Write about how much you care for, love and respect yourself.

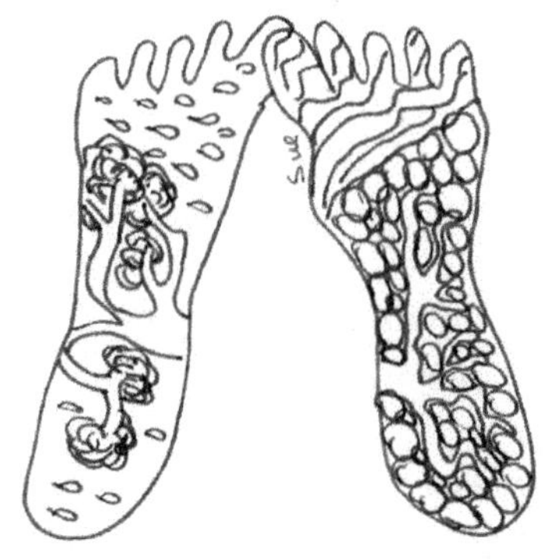

METHOD 4: EXFORM WITH DRAWING

You do not have to be an artist to do this exercise.

This exercise helps your unconscious mind reveal images that will release what is out of your awareness, but affecting you. The images can give you insights into new wisdom. Take some plain paper and some coloured pens, pencils, crayons or paint. Be free to choose whatever works for you. Keep it simple. If you have colouring pencils, use them. Don't make an excuse that you do not have any coloured pens; you can use a pen or a pencil. You are not making art.

Until you become used to giving up control, take the pen in your non-dominant hand. For example, if you are right-handed, take a pencil in your left hand.

Set an intention for your higher self or your inner guru to communicate with you through imagery and metaphor.

Examples:

- Create an intention to be free to communicate with an image about the feeling, thoughts or actions you wish to understand
- Create an intention to release that feeling through the drawing and bring yourself into a peaceful state about the event
- Create an intention to be free to draw whatever your hand wants to draw

Draw freely.

Let your body and your hand do the drawing, not your mind!

Draw whatever comes. When you feel the drawing is finished, stop.

Reflect on the drawing. Look at the drawing. Connect with the drawing as if the drawing could speak to you. What would it say? Is there a message?

Look back over your notes from any of the exercises. Have you noticed the beginning of any patterns? Have you noticed your triggers? Have you noticed your beliefs? Are they true? If they are not true, what is the truth now for you?

Do three drawings altogether.

The first drawing is to receive a message about your emotional state of being.

The second drawing is to clarify the message.

The third drawing is to ask if there is an action you need to take based on new beliefs or new truths you have discovered.

Journal

What actions will you take that create loving boundaries of self-respect?

METHOD 5: YOUR OWN WAY OF EXFORMING

Do you have your own way of exforming? Some examples:

Running

Walking

Swimming

Singing

Tai chi

Kick-boxing.

These are all respectful ways to exform and release pent-up emotion in your body.

Dumping your negative emotions onto someone else, or yourself, is being disrespectful to both yourself and them.

Choose one of the ways I have suggested to exform and understand emotions that are causing you concern.

"Nothing ever goes away until it
has taught us what we know."
Pema Chodron[21]

21 https://www.goodreads.com/quotes/593844-nothing-ever-goes-away-until-it-has-taught-us-what

WHAT YOU LEARNT

You can apply the above exercises to any situation where you feel some form of discontent or any feeling that you want to release.

Replace the word 'anger' with any word that triggers something that needs to be resolved, for example:

Frustration

Resentment

Boredom

Fear

Meanness

Annoyance

Selfishness

Greed

Envy.

Look back over your notes. Have you noticed something you or someone else does that triggers an emotion needing resolution?

When you do some of the exercises, have you now become neutral when you hear, sense, and see the triggers? If not, practise exforming, and day by day learn to speak up and create loving, respectful boundaries.

NOTE: Your Joy

You can also use the exercises of journalling, singing, dancing, walking, dancing, drawing, moving to amplify and sense what is positive in your life. Sense your aliveness, your joy, happiness, peace, grace, ease and contentment.

Make notes on your discoveries, how you are changing and what you intend on doing to learn from an emotional or physical sensory state in the future.

Journal

My triggers:

The consequences to me and others:

What will I do differently?

What else do I need to learn and practise?

What changes are happening?

lean in and listen to the world through your body

The Third Rite of Passage— New Navigation Guides

This section contains guides to help with your exploration.

These are intended to evoke you to notice, sense, play, move, imagine and intuit new ways to discover self-knowledge.

These exercises have been successful for many people, however, be aware, they may not work for you. For example, perhaps, you will not be able to sense joy, as you are filled with sadness and need to grieve before you can sense some joy in your daily life.

If you do uncover something that is uncomfortable or you do not understand, please seek out the professional support you need.

> There are three classes of people. Those who see. Those who see when they are shown. Those who do not see.
> —Leonardo da Vinci

If you are reading this book, I am sure you are one of the first two!

WHAT'S YOUR STARTING POINT?

Are you aware of the messages from your body?

Can you read them as an inner language to guide you to your wellbeing?

The purpose of the guides in this section of the book is to guide you to increase your awareness of your own inner body language. Check how aware you are now. Come back in the future and check to see if you have increased your awareness. I invite you to write some notes about what you have discovered.

Your awareness

Rate your level of awareness of your body's messages.

Start Date:

Low									High
1	2	3	4	5	6	7	8	9	10
○	○	○	○	○	○	○	○	○	○

Check in to see what you are sensing at a date in the future.

Date:

Low									High
1	2	3	4	5	6	7	8	9	10
○	○	○	○	○	○	○	○	○	○

What are you noticing now? Write some notes about how you are making sense of the messages from your body.

Date:

Low									High
1	2	3	4	5	6	7	8	9	10
○	○	○	○	○	○	○	○	○	○

What are you noticing and sensing now? Write some notes about how you are making sense of the messages from your body.

GUIDE 1: BODY SCANNING

There is much wisdom in your body, listen in, sense, intuit your inner language.

Practise daily body scanning at any time of the day to come back into your body and to increase awareness of the rich, untapped, physical sensory information within your body.

This body scan can be done in seconds, or you can spend as long as you like in any one session to explore the connection between your thoughts and your physical sensory body.

It can be done wherever you are, eyes open, standing, sitting or walking anywhere. Use it as an exercise to get to know your body, reconnect with your instincts, the sensations in your body and your feelings. It is often useful to do this body scan, or another activity you may already be doing regularly, until you get very quick at sensing your wellbeing.

On my website you can purchase an audio guided version of this exercise and others.

The long version

Sit comfortably in a chair that can support your arms, with your feet flat on the floor, legs uncrossed, hands either resting face down on your thighs or on the armrest, or together in your lap, one on top of the other, open with palms up. If you prefer to sit on the floor, sit on a cushion with your knees on the floor, or with your back against a wall and legs crossed without strain. Make sure your back is straight and, if necessary, fully supported with pillows. Allow your head to balance itself on your spine while you are looking straight ahead. Lower your chin slightly and close your eyes.

Gently become aware of your breathing, feeling the breath moving in and out of your body. Allow your breathing to settle down to its own natural rhythm. Then become aware of sensations in your body, allowing your awareness to move over the following regions (stay at each part of the body for a few breaths at least, or longer if you wish).

- Forehead, face and then the rest of your head: notice any tingling, pressure, or any other sensation at all. Soften around the eyes, let go of tension over the face, allow your jaw to drop, feel the tongue resting in the mouth...

- Neck, throat, shoulders, arms and hands: feel the shoulders letting go, feel the weight of the arms and hands resting on your legs...

- Chest area, around the heart, upper back ...

- Stomach, lower back: let go of any tension around the stomach—feel it sag and become softer. Let go of any tension around the back, allow yourself to rest into the chair or cushion...

- Hips, legs and feet: let the feet rest into the floor, becoming heavier and heavier.

You may wish to go through your body again, this time noticing if there have been any changes in sensations in any location.

When you are ready, gradually become aware of the sounds around you again, then of your whole body. In your own time, gently come out of the meditation and open your eyes, remaining in your balanced state for a short while. Move slowly to maintain the feeling of being present in your body.

The short version

Once you have practised body scanning, you can do this quickly anywhere to check your energy and your body's responses to events, people and activities.

Choose to run your attention over your entire body from the top of your head to your neck, shoulders, back, front, legs and feet. Stop where your attention notices the strongest body sensation.

Making sense of the messages in your body and accessing your inner wisdom develops through additional mind-body practices.

Practising with your choices

Practise your body scanning skills with two different kinds of choices you need to make today:

1. A small choice, for example, choosing what to have for breakfast or what clothes to wear.

2. A major choice, for example, what you want to do with your life/career, whether you want to continue spending time doing a particular activity or being with a particular person, or something else with an ongoing impact.

A small daily choice

Initially, when learning to notice and sense a new awareness you may consciously take a little more time. When you become accustomed to noticing and sensing qualities in your whole body/mind/energy you can make sense of your awareness in moments.

1. Think about your choice and consider three options. Imagine each option playing out as if you are an actor in a movie.

2. Notice your physical sensory responses to each choice. What feels like a 'yes', a 'no', a 'maybe', or a pretence?

3. Notice what you feel about each option.

Now, choose powerfully what you feel, sense, and imagine is 'right' for you—whichever imagined action created the feeling of calling out to you to take to restore your well-being.

This is a brief introduction to three additional ways to make powerful choices for yourself, and your life, and sense a powerful 'yes' or 'no' to choices in your life.

GUIDE 2: AN EMBODIED VISION

Many people create vision boards, set goals and do all kinds of future planning exercises.

Did you know that there is a high percentage of dreams, plans and visions that fall by the wayside a short time after they have been declared?

More often than not, these plans are 'out there'—outside of us and in the future. We forget that it is the things that we feel and embody that propel us into having the energy to take the action to create our dreams now in the present moment. Not to just plan and think about them, but to actually take the actions and be right now who we want to be.

Did you know that you can activate all of your senses to bring your visions to life now?

Have fun with this exercise to embody your vision or project, bringing it into the present and giving it shape. This is a way of living into something you are about to do or want, and having the experience in your whole body right now.

It is a bit like trying it on. When you do this, you will also get a feel for whether this is really something you want. Take 5–10 minutes to embody something that you wish to create.

Live in service of VISION

This exercise is best done being guided. Either ask a buddy a read the exercise aloud and take it in turns, or purchase the audio exercise from the website www.deblange.com.

Enjoy!

Embodying a future project exercise

What you are about to do...

is to engage the sensory pattern of the mind,
as well as energising the hormones in your
body to feel and sense the energy you need to
stick to the project you were thinking about.
This is the experience of activating
the body-mind systems in service to
a higher purpose and destiny.
It works because below the surface crust
of ordinary consciousness, the creative
mind is working all the time, waiting
for you to tap into it. Your deep mind
is in a state of ongoing creativity.
—Jean Houston[22]

First, find about 5–10 minutes to turn off your phone and put aside all your distractions except for what you are reading right now. Sit quietly somewhere comfortable.

Think about your vision for the next 90 days, the next year, 5 years, 10 years, or think about one particular project within your vision. You may have developed a vision board—if so, get it out and look at your board or identify one part that you would like to clearly embody right now.

Now I'm going to show you how to use your inward imagery and all of your senses to activate this project. It helps you not only finish the project but allows you to do it in a way that fits into your picture of the world.

You will want to pause after each sentence to really work with the imagined sense. You can also close your eyes after reading each sentence if it feels more focused for you that way.

22 Dr Jean Houston, www.jeanhouston.com

IMAGINE

Now, to start, I would like you to imagine you are tasting a sweet, juicy apple. Go ahead and imagine in every detail what the sensation is like on your teeth, your tongue, and inside your mouth.

Next, I want you to taste a spoonful of vanilla ice cream, strawberries and pancakes. Go ahead and imagine in every detail what the sensation is like on your teeth, your tongue, and inside your mouth.

Now, hot-buttered toast.

Now taste the extravagant celebratory meal you will eat after your project is finished, with all your favourite foods. Imagine and sense every detail.

SMELL

Next, I want you to smell a pine forest, gum trees or cut grass after a summer rain shower. Imagine and sense every detail. Imagine the smell is right under your nose

Now, a thick pine forest. Imagine and sense every detail.

Freshly baked bread. Imagine and sense every detail.

Imagine that your project has a smell. A smell in the beginning, a different smell during the project, and another smell at the end of the project. Now smell your project after it's finished (don't worry about the logic of that, just imagine what it smells like).

TOUCH

Now I want you to touch the bony softness of a horse's nose. Imagine and sense every detail.

Next, wade through a tub of warm honey that touches your skin and sticks to your feet and legs.

Clap your hands and play pat-a-cake with a small child. Notice a different feeling when you touch your hands and the child's hands.

Touch your project with your hands and other parts of your body, roll on your project, lie down on your project, hug your project as it is being completed.

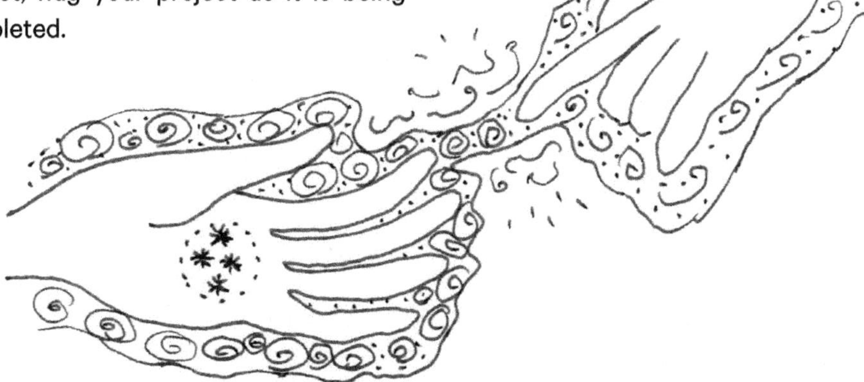

SEE

Now I want you to see a sunrise.

A sunset.

A falling star.

A good friend's face as they are looking at you.

Now I want you to see your project being accomplished.

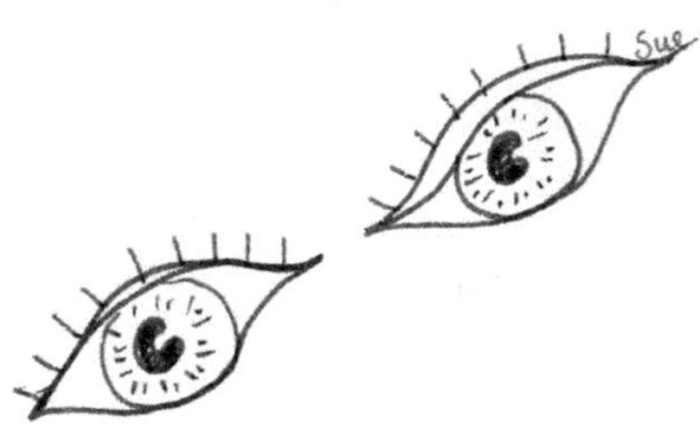

HEAR

I want you to hear the sound of a rainstorm on your roof.

Hear an opera singer holding her highest note.

Hear Martin Luther King giving his "I have a dream" speech.

Now hear something that has to do with the accomplishment of your project.

FINISH

Take a deep breath and run your project through all the senses again: taste, touch, smell, sight, sound. Go ahead and take ten seconds to do so.

You may wish to draw your project now or embellish your vision board after doing this exercise.

REVIEW

Does your body feel that this project is essential for your well-being?

If not, has a different project surfaced? Or have you created a connection with this project that has inspired you to take the action you need?

You can do this exercise at any time of the year when you want to embody a project or embody any part of your vision and bring it into your whole body reality.

What happened to how you felt about your vision or project when you did this exercise?

Do you have a photo of your drawing or vision board? Pin it on the 'Embodying Your Vision' board on Pinterest.

NEXT STEPS

Create a #senses quest. Use the following guides to notice your energy, understand the power of the language you use, partner with your inner crew and activate your senses.

Then return to your vision and see what part of your vision you have embodied.

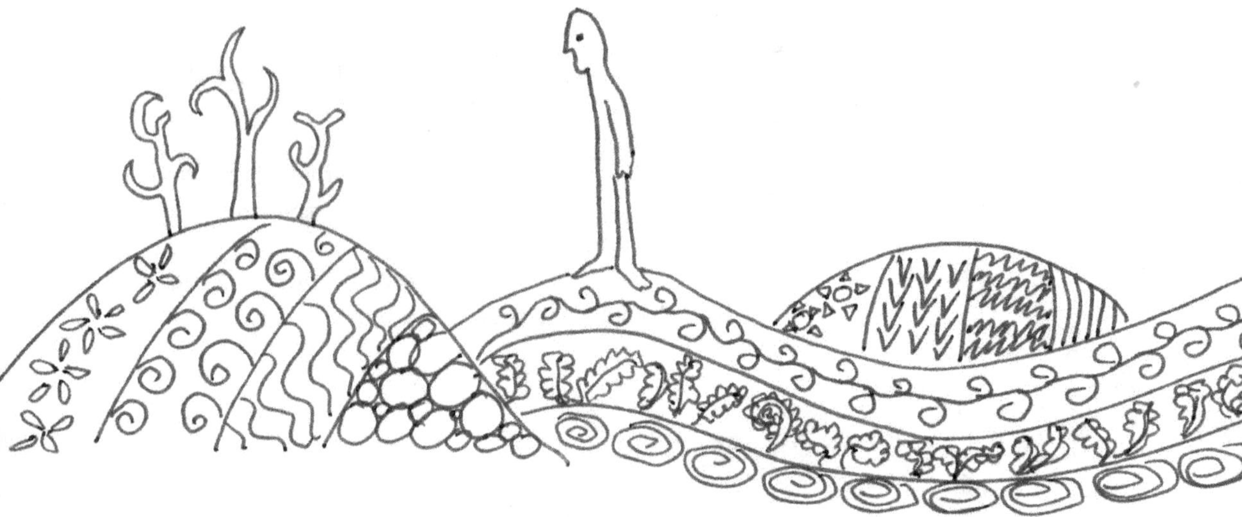

GUIDE 3: NOTICING YOUR ENERGY

This is an invitation to notice what gives you energy and what takes your energy away. This is a choice, your choice. If you do this, you will begin to notice things that you have never noticed before.

What can you notice? Your energy is expressed through your body as physical sensations such as:

Tingling

Tension

Elasticity

Tightness.

Your energy is also expressed via your senses: in smell, taste, touch, sight, hearing, feeling, temperature, and in those physical sensations we interpret as concepts and ways of being, for example, feeling:

Stuck

Flow

Control

Freedom

Resilience.

We often interpret these sensations as emotions:

Boredom, apathy

Tiredness, exhaustion

Frustration, anxiety, confusion

Fear, under threat

Sadness, grief, depression

Happiness, joy, elation

Anger, rage, upset

Contentment, satisfaction, safety

Love, peace

Shame, guilt, vulnerability.

The more you notice, the more you will notice, and soon you will notice patterns in the things that give you energy and the things that take your energy away. When you see patterns, you can then choose wisely what actions are more fulfilling. Often we make choices based on what other people tell us or on limited information, as we do not look long enough to notice the patterns. If you choose my invitation, you will see new patterns to help your choices in life.

An invitation to notice your energy

Either fill in the blank spaces in this book or get yourself a journal and use the headings from the exercise. Take one of the topics each day and jot down notes. You can add more topics yourself.

How frequently will you notice and use a journal? That is your choice.

Jotting down notes will help you see when there is something that occurs once or something that is repeated. It is the things that repeat themselves in your life that you want to start to attend to. If you notice something happens frequently and it is positive, affirm yourself. If you notice something that depletes you regularly, you can choose to stop or do less of that activity.

The next step is to work out what belief you hold about yourself that you are doing something that is taking energy your away. This process is one step at a time. There is more about how to do this and what to look for in my other work in articles and blogs on beliefs and self-care.

To see how much you increase your awareness, have a baseline and take 30 minutes to answer the questions that follow in the guidebook before you begin the process of day-by-day noticing. This will help you see what you are noticing that you did not know before.

Over a period of time that you designate, take one area and write some notes. Make a commitment to pause and notice something about your energy once a day. Then you can practise noticing something new for the rest of your life.

HOW TO NOTICE YOUR ENERGY

Let's begin with these topics. (You can add your own.). After the list, there is more information about each topic.

1. Breathing
2. Your body
3. Your environment
4. Technology
5. People
6. Add your own topic
7. Review
8. Work
9. Stillness
10. Mind
11. Time
12. Spirituality
13. Add your own topic
14. Review

Keep noticing. Make this a lifelong habit.

1. Breathing

Yes, breathing. Notice your breath.

When we are stressed or anxious, we have a natural reaction to shorten and tighten our breathing. We breathe into our upper body rather than deep into our belly. Short tight breaths do not give our cells the oxygen they need, and if we keep on taking short breaths, we will become more and more anxious and stressed. Just noticing your breathing and taking deeper, slower breaths can have a significant effect on our energy levels.

What I know now:

My intention for today is to notice:

What energised me today was:

What I responded to with lowered my energy and interest was:

2. My Body

Do a quick body scan and notice what your body is feeling at any time during the day.

Notice what you are feeling. High energy? Low energy? Something in between? Or perhaps dull? Excited? If you cannot detect a feeling, then notice your body sensations. Perhaps there is tightness in your shoulders or gurgling in your stomach. Begin to notice such things as sensations, textures, shapes, strength, weakness, colours, sounds and scents.

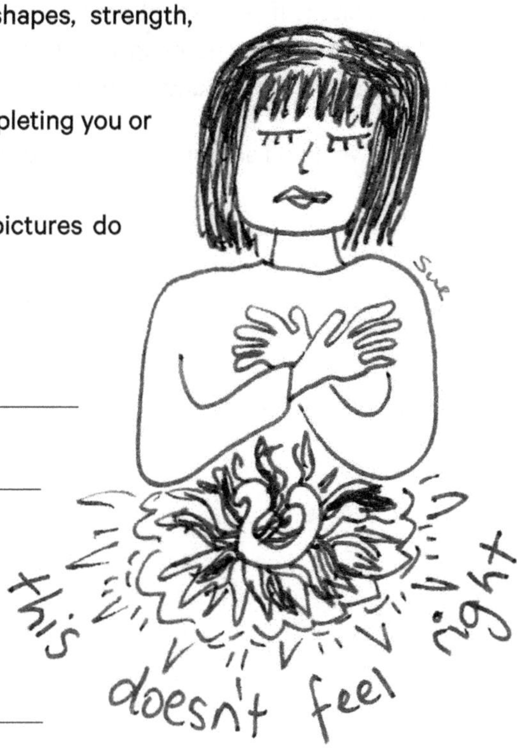

Notice what you are thinking. Are your thoughts depleting you or energising you?

Notice what you are imagining. What images or pictures do you have of an activity?

What I know now:

My intention for today is to notice:

What energised me today was:

What I responded to with lowered my energy and interest was:

3. Your Environment

Notice how your body feels when you walk into a room, a building, along the footpath, across the park, at the beach, in a forest, in a car, on a bike, anywhere. Play, be curious and notice as if it was the first time you were there.

Notice what you are feeling. High energy? Low energy? Something in between? Or perhaps dull? Excited? If you cannot detect a feeling, notice your body sensations. Is there tightness in your shoulders or gurgling in your stomach? Notice sensations, textures, shapes, strength, weakness, colours, sounds and scents.

Notice what you are thinking. Are your thoughts depleting you or energising you?

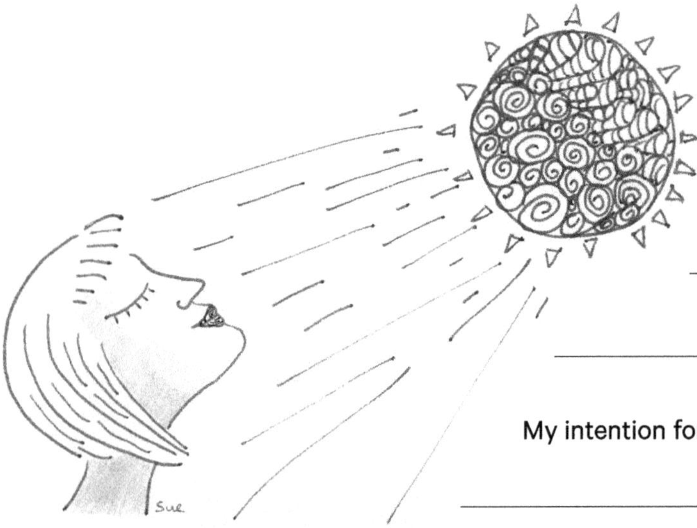

Notice what you are imagining. What images or pictures spring to mind when you are in a specific location?

What I know now:

My intention for today is to notice:

What energised me today was:

What I responded to with lowered my energy and interest was:

4. Technology

We live in a society where we are constantly streaming information from tablets, computers, TV, smartphones, and more. Do they take your energy away? Do they energise you? Do you know? How long before you are tired? What do you do to replenish yourself after a long period in front of a screen?

Notice what you are feeling. High energy? Low energy? Something in between? Or perhaps dull? Excited? Notice such things as sensations, textures, shapes, strength, weakness, colours, sounds and scents.

Notice what you are thinking. Are your thoughts depleting you or energising you?

Notice what you are imagining.

What I know now:

____

____

My intention for today is to notice:

____

____

What energised me today was:

____

____

What I responded to with lowered my energy and interest was:

____

____

5. People

Have you ever been around people who are bundles of energy? Do they tire you? Do they give you energy? What do you do when you notice your energy is drained away when you are with someone? Do you stay and suffer or do you excuse yourself, take care of yourself and move away? Just begin to notice. What do you do when you notice your energy is lifted?

Notice what you are feeling. High energy? Low energy? Something in between? Or perhaps dull? Excited? Notice such things as sensations, textures, shapes, strength, weakness, colours, sounds and scents.

Notice what you are thinking. Are your thoughts depleting you or energising you?

Notice what you are imagining.

What images or pictures spring to mind when you are with specific people?

What I know now:

____

____

My intention for today is to notice:

____

____

What energised me today was:

____

____

What I responded to with lowered my energy and interest was:

____

____

6. Review

Look back over your notes. Have you noticed the beginning of any patterns? Any particular situations or stimuli that cause a reaction of increasing your energy or lowering your energy.

Jot down what you think, feel and imagine might be the beginning of a pattern. Choose any of the areas that have caught your attention.

What keeps repeating? What am I noticing?

7. Your Own Topic

Choose one of the areas where you thought that a pattern may be emerging. Go back to this area and look more specifically.

For example, if you are noticing your energy changes with different people, pick one person who you will be with today and be even more curious. Perhaps you have pinpointed that you have a defensive reaction and feel like retreating when this person speaks.

Look again.

This time you may notice your reaction is triggered by a voice tone, the language the person uses, or something else.

Or perhaps you notice your energy being uplifted, being excited or being peaceful.

Look again.

What is your body responding to? This time you may notice your body responds to the eye contact, touch, the story, the invitation to participate, the interest in you.

There is no right or wrong answer. Your experience is unique to you. Notice and collect information to see if a pattern emerges. You are on a quest looking for what your body responds to that creates coherence, and what your body responds to that creates a disruption of some kind. This does not mean disruptions are to be avoided. Rather disruptions are often a gift. They are the opportunity to check in with our assumptions. We may have false beliefs about ourselves that lead to us responding in certain ways.

Check in with the responses in your body to see if any of these are the cause:

- What a person is saying or doing
- How a person is saying or doing what they are doing
- A memory of a similar event that has nothing to do with the present has been triggered.

When you see a pattern emerging, you can go to the next step of uncovering your assumptions, values and beliefs. The last step is to choose a loving action for yourself.

Begin the exploration of noticing the energy in your body.

What revitalises me?

What takes my energy away?

What do I know now about this pattern?

I have noticed these triggers:

I have noticed these are my responses:

I have noticed these are the consequences:

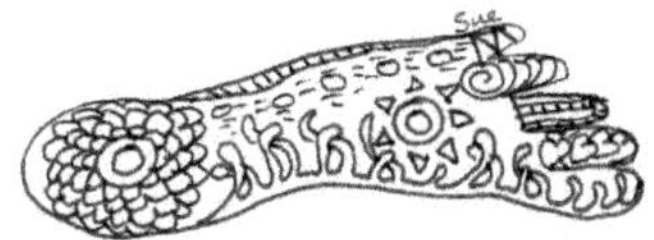

8. Work

What is the story you create about work? How does that story affect you and your work?

Do you take far longer to do what you know you could do in less time as you have low energy?

Or when you do complete work, you are given meaningless jobs to do that make you even more stressed and tired? Notice what happens to your energy during the day.

Notice what you are feeling. High energy? Low energy? Something, in between? Or perhaps dull? Excited? If you cannot detect a feeling, then notice your body sensations. Begin to notice such things as sensations, textures, shapes, strength, weakness, colours, sounds and scents.

Notice what you are thinking. Are your thoughts depleting you or energising you?

Notice what you are imagining.

What images or pictures spring to mind when you are with specific people?

My intention for today is to notice:

____

____

What energised me today was:

____

____

What I responded to with lowered my energy and interest was:

____

____

9. Stillness

When was the last time you took a walk in the fresh air without rushing to an appointment?

When was the last time you sat on a park bench, mused and noticed the clouds rolling over, the birds in the sky, the buds forming on the trees, or the leaves falling?

When was the last time you sat down and had a slow meal, cooking and enjoying the luscious tastes, smells and feasting on the delight of colours and textures of the food as you cooked and ate?

What I know now about being still or not being still:

My intention for today is to notice what happens if I take time to be still:

What energised me today was:

What I responded to with lowered my energy and interest was:

10. Mind

Everyone has different things that give them energy or take energy away, but many of us do not take time to notice what these things are, and adjust what we spend our time doing accordingly. When we do not consciously choose the actions that benefit us, we end up stressed, depressed or confused. The same can apply for thoughts.

What thoughts do you have that increase anxiety? Who is the voice inside your head? Do you know?

What thoughts do you have that lift your spirits?

My intention for today is to notice:

____

____

What energised me today was:

____

____

What I responded to with lowered my energy and interest was:

____

____

11. Time

Are there different times of the day when you have different levels of energy? Do you wake up feeling tired and need to have that cup of coffee to get you out of bed and into the commuter? Are you drowsy mid-afternoon and falling asleep at your desk? Do you have times when time slips away as you are so immersed in what you are doing?

Take note of these times and what you are doing. Notice what you are feeling. High energy? Low energy? Something in between? Or perhaps dull? Excited? If you cannot detect a feeling, notice sensations, textures, shapes, strength, weakness, colours, sounds and scents.

Notice what you are thinking. Are your thoughts depleting you or energising you? Notice what you are imagining. What images do you have when you think about how much time you have?

What I know now about time:

____

____

____

My intention for today is to notice:

____

____

What energised me today was:

____

____

What I responded to with lowered my energy and interest was:

____

____

12. Spirituality

What do you do that connects you to something bigger than yourself? Music, nature, walking, drawing, writing, surfing, painting, patting a dog, singing to elderly people, helping in a homeless shelter? Do these things nurture you? If not, what does?

How do you take the time to nourish your soul?

My intention for today is to notice my body/spirit:

____

____

My intention for today is to notice:

____

____

What energised me today was:

____

____

What I responded to with lowered my energy and interest was:

____

____

13. Add Your Own Topic

Choose one of the areas where you thought that a pattern may be emerging and has caught your attention. Go back to this area and look more specifically.

For example, if you are noticing your energy with people and one person triggers a strong response, either positive or negative, choose that person and be curious at noticing what is happening that triggers a response. See if you can pinpoint a defensive reaction. Do you feel like retreating when this person speaks? Do you feel energised when this person walks into the room?

Look again.

This time notice if your reaction is triggered by voice tone, language, or something else. Or perhaps you notice your energy being uplifted, being excited or being peaceful.

Look again.

What is your body responding to? This time you may notice your body responds to eye contact, touch, the story, the invitation to participate, or the interest in you.

There is no right or wrong answer. Your experience is unique to you. Notice and collect information to see if a pattern emerges. You are on a quest looking for what your body responds to that creates coherence and what your body responds to that creates a disruption of some kind. This does not mean disruptions are to be avoided. Rather disruptions are often a gift. They are the opportunity to check in with our assumptions and see what else we still have to learn.

We may have false beliefs about ourselves that lead us to responding in certain ways.

Check in with what your body is responding to. Check in to see if it is what this person is saying/doing or how they are saying/doing it, or have they triggered a memory of a past event that has nothing to do with the present.

When you see a pattern emerging, go to the next step. Look at your response. Uncover your assumptions, values and beliefs. Choose a loving action for yourself and develop new strategies and skills to increase your body wisdom. Find out more about how to do this in my additional eBooks, articles and services.

First things first: begin with noticing. Your body is a storehouse of sensory information from your birth, your genealogy and your experiences. Your cells have a memory of a long time past. You are learning to notice the memory in your cells via your senses, your energy and your emotions.

14. Review

Look back over your notes. Have you noticed the beginning of any patterns?

Jot down what you think, feel and imagine might be the beginning of a pattern. Choose any of the areas that have caught your attention.

My patterns:

My triggers:

The consequences:

What I will do differently:

The consequences of doing or saying something different:

What else I need to learn:

What changes am I noticing?

YOUR PATTERNS

Today's focus is to notice how your patterns manifest.

What I already know about my patterns:

What energised me today was

I noticed the trigger for being energised was:

What lowered my energy and interest was

I noticed the trigger for lowered energy and interest was:

What patterns are emerging?

What am I choosing to do differently?

What changes are happening?

This is a work in progress. Keep noticing, keep practising, one skill at a time.

Have fun.

Be an explorer.

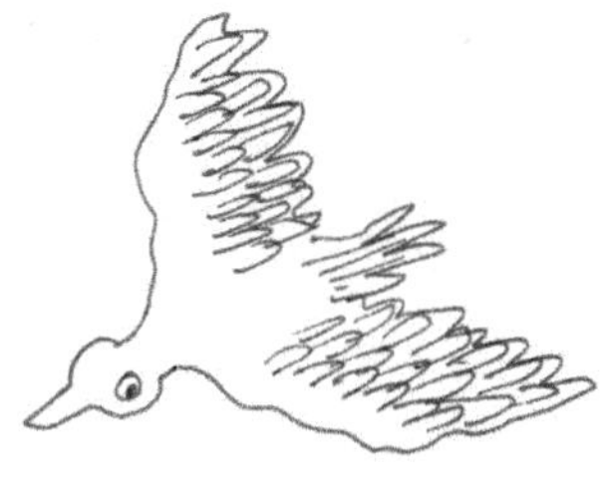

GUIDE 4: NOTICING YOUR LANGUAGE

You know we all have voices in our head. Some of them drive you nuts, some are wise and some are funny. Can you imagine a new way of relating to your inner voices?

What would you call them if you imagined they are on your team, working and playing with you to advise, guide and support you in life and work? I call mine my inner crew.

This week, notice the different voices, name them, invite them to tea with you and get to know them—even the voices you may call your saboteur. Often the ones that sabotage us are really voices we have embodied from an authority figure from long ago. Get to know them, ask the ones that are not your truth what beliefs you took on that you embodied in your being, when you were unaware that is what you were doing. Ask them what you need to give yourself now, so they can to go back to their rightful home and you can live what is your truth and bring fulfilment and peace to yourself.

I was coaching a client, who I will call Tina. She called her negative judgemental voice her 'Beastie'. I invited her to imagine this 'Beastie' was a part of herself with a message and a gift. As long as she was seeing her 'Beastie' as not a part of her, she was fighting with herself. Of course, 'Beastie' would not stop causing problems for Tina until 'Beastie' was understood. 'Beastie' would amplify herself when Tina ignored her, or put a lid on her, just like a child amplifies what she is saying when she is ignored. When Tina hated 'Beastie', she was hating a part of herself. 'Beastie' would surface and say, "What about me? You are not listening to me."

When you are filled with self-loathing, you don't bring out the best in yourself.

I invited Tina to get to know 'Beastie', to find out where 'Beastie' came from and find out how she could partner with 'Beastie' to navigate her life well. I invited her to see that in the voice of 'Beastie' was a gift, a message about something she was supposed to be giving herself but was not, and that is why 'Beastie' was appearing—to cry out, "What are you doing to me? I am yours but you are not taking care of me. I am hurting because you are hating me."

Tina had a chat and sensed what 'Beastie' felt. 'Beastie' told her she appeared when Tina was not being loving to herself. She was literally being a beast to herself. She asked 'Beastie' what she needed to feel loved, cared for and accepted.

Beastie said she needed to be totally loved and accepted by Tina for everything she was and everything she was not; to give up comparing herself with others and judging herself against others. Tina needed to learn how to nurture herself rather than expecting her partner to give her the nurturing she needed. She needed to 'grow up' and become an adult who could take care of herself. She needed to stop pushing and pulling on her partner like an adolescent pulls and pushes on a parent as they are learning to take responsibility for themselves.

Tina developed a new relationship with 'Beastie' and re-named her 'Beautiful One'. She created a loving relationship of respect with herself. She realised Beastie had surfaced from an authority figure earlier in her life, who had always told her she was not good enough and compared her with the other children in her class whom she thought were more beautiful and more intelligent. Tina put Beastie to rest and became her 'Beautiful One', living into a new freedom and expression of her true self.

NAME YOUR INNER CREW

Reflection and naming

This week, notice your inner crew—the voices inside your head. Sense inside your body the different parts of you. Name them. Invite them to talk to you. Be curious. Ask them what their gift to you is.

Playfully explore

Images

Create a picture of your inner crew. See them as a team who support one another in an interdependent relationship and who help you to effectively navigate your life and be the best that you can be.

Dancing

Dance with your inner crew. Do they want to tango, yet you constrain yourself? Do they want to do Tai chi, yet you are always doing rock n' roll?

Nature

How does being in nature bring out different parts of you? Which members of your inner crew shines in nature?

Music

Do different parts of your inner crew respond differently to music? Play by putting on different types of music and see who emerges.

Voice

Listen to your voice change throughout the day. How does it change when talking with different people, about different topics? Can you notice when a different part of you comes forth whether your voice tone changes? What voices do the different characters have? Can you pick up who has surfaced with a different voice tone? The judge, the critic, the nurturer, the wise sage, the innocent child or the rebellious adolescent may each sound different in pitch, volume, speed and even word choice.

Nourishing your inner crew

Different parts of ourselves have different insights and different needs, and are nourished in different ways.

Which needs are you ignoring, or forgetting are there? Which ones get all the nourishment at the expense of the others? Are you letting one drown out the rest?

Are you handing over the rudder to one that does not have the skills and strategies to take you where you want to go?

Invite a wise, nourishing inner crew to be present for you. Who would you like to call on?

Your wise old woman?

Your nurturer?

Your adventurer?

Your creative soul?

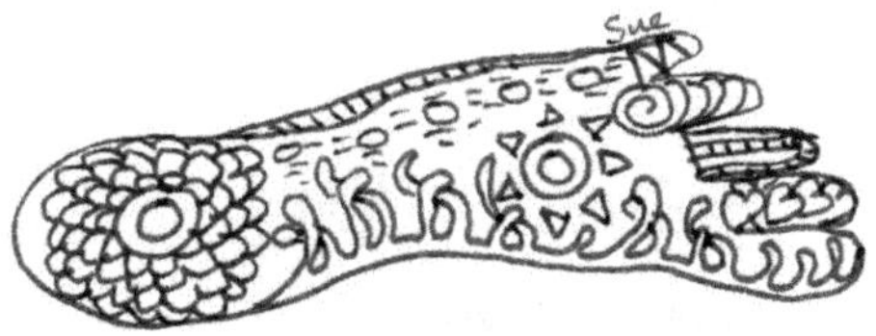

GUIDE: 4 BODY PLAY[23]

I invite you to explore and notice your body movements. The way your body moves tells you about what it needs, what you are blocking, and what it needs to sense inner freedom, creativity, joy and peace.

Hanging, swinging, thrusting, shape and stillness

Throughout the day, notice whether you are:

Hanging

Swinging

Thrusting

Moving slowly

Being still.

Play with different movements. Pay attention to when your body changes and notice the energy in different movements and shapes.

A core body wisdom skill is body scanning. You have been invited to do regular body scans and observe what happens when you notice your body without trying to control or change

23 I learnt many body play exercises from Cynthia Winton-Henry and Phil Porter from InterPlay

anything—unless your body naturally shifts. I also invite you to give your body freedom to change if it needs to in the way it needs. Learn to give your body the freedom to express itself without controlling it and learn to understand what your body is asking for.

While this is a lifelong process, playing with different movements and the energy of those movements is a great way to get started. Try this exercise.

Create an intention. For example: "I am learning to notice the language of my body."

When you think and talk about your intention, notice:

- How your body is shaped
- What your body is feeling
- Your voice tone
- Your energy
- Other people's energy when you talk about your intention
- Other people's body shape and voice tone when you talk about your intention.

Use this as a baseline. Now when you say and think your intention, give your body the freedom to express that intention with each different type of movement:

Hanging. Swinging. Thrusting. Slow. Still.

What happens?

Which of the movements give energy to or take energy away from your intention?

Which of the movements evoked a creative response? An image? Something else?

What else did you notice?

If you did not have an intention, be curious and play with these different body movements and shapes throughout the day.

Notice if you are stuck in one movement or shape. Or do you switch between all 4?

What happens when you notice you are doing one movement and the person you are with is in another energy movement?

Let your body move and notice the body wisdom stored in your body movement.

Build up the data about your body wisdom. Write and draw in your journal. Over time you will see new patterns. The patterns will provide you with new knowledge about yourself so you can make powerful, intuitive choices for your life.

Here are some additional notes on the four different body shapes, energies and actions.

> *Hanging—you know the type person who is very laid back; they literally hang around.*
>
> *Swinging—then there are those who swing from activity to activity; they are light-hearted.*
>
> *Thrusting—these action-orientated types boldly move and get things done; they find it hard to hang around.*
>
> *Slow and still—then there are those of us who have taken on being still in life, people who love yoga and meditation do lots of shape and stillness.*

There is nothing wrong or right about any of these body shapes, and actions. They are all different:

> *Different energy*
>
> *Different purpose*
>
> *Different way of being.*

What if you are mainly a thruster and you have never learnt to hang around, or to swing to go along with others, or to be still?

What if you are more of a shape and stillness type of person and you are not as good at thrusting, taking bold action and getting things done, or at being laid back and at going along with others as you control your shape?

What if you prefer a body shape as a hanger? You hang around and wait for someone else to initiate and never do yourself.

And so on.

So what if this week you noticed what body movement you spend most of your time in:

> *Swinging*
>
> *Hanging*
>
> *Thrusting*
>
> *Slow and still.*

And when you notice, give yourself permission to play with one of the other types of movement and energies.

Try hanging—walk as if you are just hanging around, or being gently pulled by a big balloon in a soft breeze, just hanging at the end of a string.

Or walk with a swing, yes, swing along. Maybe your swing even turns into a skip. See how much fun you can have with swinging along. Swing your arms and your legs. Notice what happens to your face and shoulders when you swing. Do a waltz in your lounge room.

Thrust yourself forward with purpose. Walk boldly, do some karate chop movements. Throw an imaginary paint ball in the air, thrusting along.

Shape and stillness. Walk slowly with lots of stillness. Stop and smell the roses along the way. Notice being in different shapes as you stop to bend down. Look sideways, turn to look up to the sky and hold for a few moments, enjoying the embrace of the universe.

Play with your movement anywhere:

- In your lounge room
- In a park
- Walking down the street.

You can do this anywhere and be unnoticed, or you may gradually lose inhibitions and play and realise it does not matter if someone notices you. If they do, they will mirror you and start swinging along with you playfully! Or a thruster may slow down when they see you stopping and enjoying natural beauty along the way.

Anytime:

- One a day
- All four at one time.

Play and notice. Notice what happens to you and what happens to others around you.

Notice when you are one of these movements and the person with you is the same. Notice when you are in one movement and the person with you is the opposite.

Let your body move and notice the body wisdom stored in your body movement.

GUIDE 5: ENRICH OUR LIVES WITH OUR SENSES

Set an intention to be present with all of your senses in order to experience life to the full.

Why?

- Become emotionally resilient
- Tap into your intuition
- Choose actions from your heart
- Connect to your spirit
- Overcome anxiety
- Enjoy life fully in the present
- And much, much more.

A little note to begin

Replace judging yourself and others with curiosity and acceptance of what is and what is not.

Write in this document and use it as a journal or you can record your observations in your own journal.

Positive consequences

Some positive consequences of being sensory aware to the full are:

- Generating a playful attention in order to enjoy all that there is and to activate gratitude for what you have right now
- Activating all of your senses to receive rich experiences in life
- Learning to feel what is loving to you and what generates feelings of well-being
- Learning to notice what triggers anxiety, negativity, and negative self-doubt, and being able to choose to do less of those things

- Limiting how much you listen to mental chatter and the capacity to limit negative self-talk.

What senses are available to us in our physical, sensory capacity?

We are so lucky to have....

Sense 1: Vision

Seeing what is external from our eyes; colour, texture, shape, movement, light, shadow. Describes the ability of the brain and the eye in detecting electromagnetic waves within the visible range (light) and interpreting the image as 'sight'.

Internal vision: seeing internal images from the past, present and future.

Sense 2: Hearing

Noises external to ourselves. Hearing: noises, music, voices inside our head and body. Sound perception results from tiny hair fibres in the inner ear, detecting the motion of a membrane, which vibrates in response to changes in the pressure.

Sense 3: Taste

From our mouth and tongue. Taste is one of the two main 'chemical' senses. The four well-known taste receptors detect sweet, salt, sour, and bitter.

Sense 4: Smell

Through your nose; scents in the present moment that bring back memories of past moments.

Sense 5: Touch

What do you have permission to touch? Pat your dog, feel satin sheets, hold a hand.

Being 'touched': by something that is a felt presence, a heart connection.

Sense 6: Thermoception (thermal)

Sensing the presence of heat and the absence of heat (cold) by the skin, including internal skin passages.

Sense 7: Nocipection (physiological pain)

The non-conscious perception of nerve-damage or damage to tissue.

Sense 8: Balance

Our perception of balance and acceleration is related to our inner ear cavities containing fluid.

Sense 9: Movement

Sensing our bodies as they move, as well as movement in our environment.

Sense 10: Propioception (the kinaesthetic sense)

Our perception of body awareness—we rely on this enormously, but we are frequently not aware.

Sense 11: Intuition

Sensing our gut feelings; sensing energy in our bodies, in others and in the environment

Sense 12: Voice

Our voice tone, breadth of pitch, volume and emotional state that affects the resonance of our voice.

YOUR SENSES

Once a day for the next 14 days, focus on activating senses with different activities during the day. You can use the following examples as a guide or replace these activities with ones that suit you.

Spend approximately 5–10 minutes fully activating and deepening your physical sensory awareness and your body's knowing.

Focus on one sense as fully as you can. You are likely to notice how the other senses are activated for a deep experience.

Before you start:

- Invite a buddy to do the exercise with you
- Share what you intend on doing with your coach or a trusted buddy
- Create it playfully.

Check in with your buddy.

Take turns to share with each other what you are noticing.

Choose to be an explorer, experiment and be curious about activating your senses to deepen your access to your intuitive body wisdom.

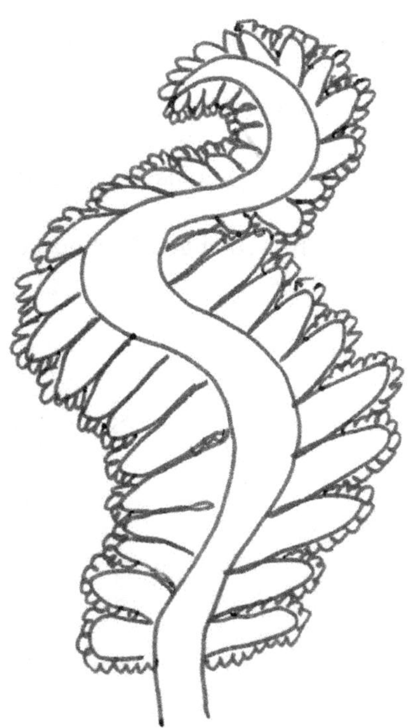

(Day 1)

In the shower or bath or at the beach or in a river

Notice your kinaesthetic awareness, what you feel in a sensory, physical way

Feel

Feel the water running over your skin starting at the top of your head. Follow the feeling from the top of your head slowly all the way down your whole body.

Feel the water as it runs into your mouth and over your face.

Feel your skin with your hands from the top of your head all the way down your whole body.

Feel the soap on your hands and feel the difference between your hand running over your body and your hand with soap running all over your body.

Feel the towel against your skin when you are drying yourself and notice the difference between your skin with water, with hands, with hands with soap, and now a towel.

Notice

Listen to the running water. Hear it through all of your body.

Smell the water, smell the soap, smell your skin.

Taste the water in your mouth.

Look at your body, the water and the room you are in. Look at shape, shadow, colour, texture.

Imagine you have all the time in the world to do this exercise, be totally immersed in it...

When you have finished, come back and write about the experience. What did you notice?

(Day 2)

A slow meal

Sensing: Taste and smell

Allow a little extra time (5–10 minutes) to eat one of your meals throughout the day. Do this on your own or ask your partner to do this with you—in silence. Except for *ooh, aaah, mmm,* avoid speaking if you can. Then share your rich experience.

Before eating, look at the colours, patterns, shapes, textures of the food.

Smell the food.

Make sure there is at least one piece of food you can hold in your hand to eat. What does this feel like on your skin, in your hand?

Take one small bite and swish the food around your mouth longer than normal; roll it on your tongue, feel the texture and wallow in the taste for as long as you can while chewing slowly.

Swallow and feel the food go down your throat into your body.

How long does it take you to feel full?

Sensing: Visual and auditory

Listen to the noise in your throat and/or your stomach.

Notice how full you are feeling while you are eating.

Finish when you feel full, or just prior to feeling full, rather than eating everything on your plate just because it is still there.

Imagine you have all the time in the world to do this exercise, be totally immersed in it...

When you have finished, come back, draw, write about the experience. What did you notice?

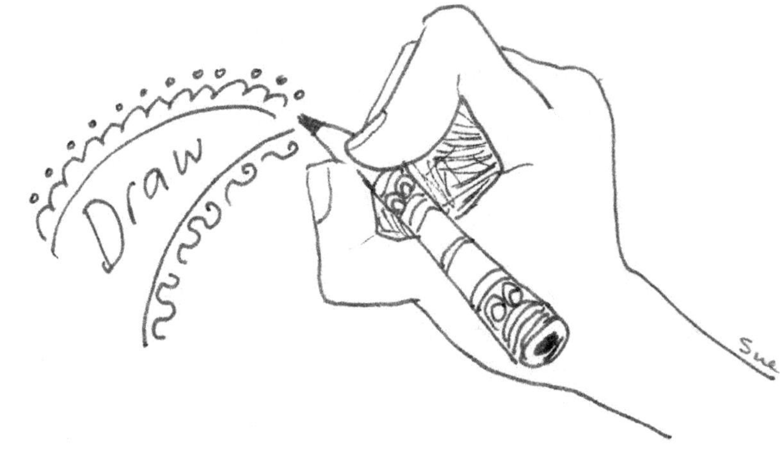

(Day 3)

Movement

Kinaesthetic sensing

Choose one time during the day when you have to walk, ride a bike, dance or exercise for approximately 5–10 minutes. This time pay attention as you are moving with all of your senses one at a time. For example, when walking:

Walk slowly for a couple of minutes and notice the following:

Notice placing your feet on the pavement or the grass. What does that feel like? Do you feel heavy? Light?

Noticing: Auditory and visual

Listen to the noises—natural and man-made—around you while you are walking.

Look around you as you are walking. See if you notice things on this path that you have never noticed before.

Walk a normal pace for a couple of minutes and see if you notice any difference.

Walk fast for a couple of minutes. See what you notice.

Imagine you have all the time in the world to do this exercise. Be totally immersed in it...

When you have finished, come back, draw and write about the experience. What did you notice?

(Day 4)

Animals

If you have an animal, spend 5–10 minutes totally exploring being with your pet. Look into your pet's eyes, gaze at the textures of its coat, feel the texture of its coat (if it is a pet that can be patted), smell the scent of your pet, talk to your pet, listen to your pet's breathing and heartbeat, watch your pet play, play with your pet, hug your pet (f it is a pet that can be hugged.)

If you do not have a pet, take time with a friend's pet, watch dogs in the park, ask someone walking their dog about their dog and if you can have a pat.

If you do not have any access to a pet, practise being fully immersed and connecting to something that creates a felt bodily experience that is enjoyable. Perhaps you practise a craft or a hobby. Take time to be fully immersed in the activity using all of your senses i.e. cooking, woodworking, sewing, drawing, painting, riding bikes, at gym, dance class, yoga.......

Imagine you have all the time in the world to do this exercise, be totally immersed in it...

When you have finished, come back, draw and write about the experience. What did you notice?

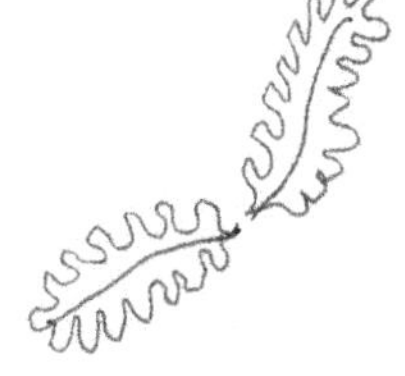

(Day 5)

Shopping

Sensing and visual noticing

Take five minutes to explore wandering in the shopping centre rather than planning where you are going. Let your body do the walking, not your mind. Where does your body feel like walking? Notice whether you will let your body move freely or whether you want to control where you want your body to go. What difference does it make if you let go for 5 minutes and play like a small child exploring?

Notice what your body is attracted to. Is it colour? Texture? Sound? Smell?

Notice what your body feels like walking away from.

Imagine you have all the time in the world to do this exercise. Be totally immersed in it...

When you have finished, come back, draw and write about the experience. What did you notice?

Nature

Do you spend time in nature? Take five minutes to activate all your senses in a natural setting. Fully watch a sunset, or a sunrise. Sit in a forest, on a grassy hill, or at the beach. Watch a bird catch a fish, or some other natural activity. Breathe in the sights, sounds, smells, taste, and textures of a natural environment.

Imagine you have all the time in the world to do this exercise. Be totally immersed in it...

When you have finished, come back, draw and write about the experience. What did you notice?

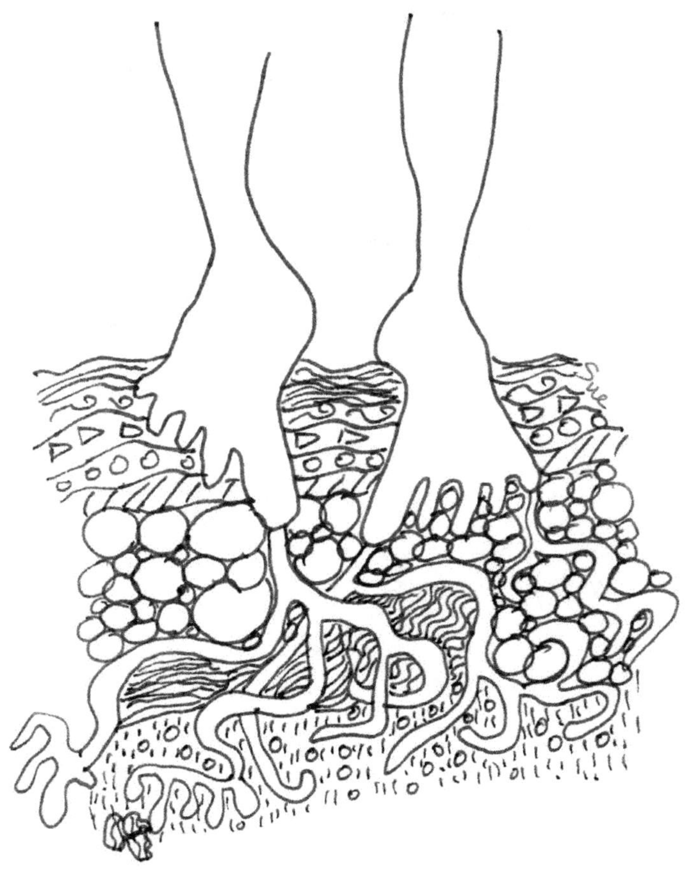

(Day 7)

Sleeping

When you go to bed, spend five minutes noticing your body.

Listen to the sounds in the room and gradually start to listen to your body. Listen to your breath, your heartbeat, your movement on the sheets.

Feel your skin on the sheets, your face on the pillow, your body on the bed.

Notice how long it takes to settle.

Notice your thoughts. If there is negative self-talk, notice it and then notice an area of your body. Notice what your body is feeling when you talk negatively. Notice your breath. Breathe out a sigh. Choose to care for yourself, tell yourself what would be loving to you and breathe out any negative self-talk.

If you are giving yourself positive self-talk, notice what your body is feeling. Breathe. Breathe in the positive energy.

Imagine you have all the time in the world to do this exercise. Be totally immersed in it...

When you have finished, come back, draw and write about the experience. What did you notice?

(Day 8)

Music

Sense: Auditory

Play some music. Close your eyes. Play with being still, relaxing into the music allowing it to impregnate every cell in your body.

Do you see images when you listen to the music?

Open your eyes, stand up, allow your body to move, to make shapes, to dance as if the music is moving you.

Is your body telling a story?

Imagine you have all the time in the world to do this exercise. Be totally immersed in it...

When you have finished, come back, draw and write about the experience. What did you notice?

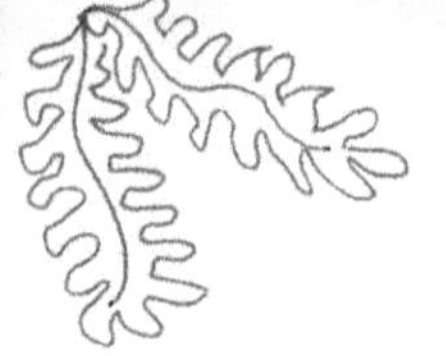

Day 9 Review

See if you are noticing life as it goes by in technicolour, richer, tastier, yummier than before you activated your senses.

This is the beginning of being in your body and heightening your senses to access the wisdom in your body. Keep practising and playing this game, or a game you made up, to enjoy the richness of all the senses you are blessed to have been born with for the rest of your life.

After seven days, what did you notice?

What does it feel like?

What are you noticing now?

Take a photo of the slow meal you enjoyed, your pet, your hobby, the sunset you watched or something that you did this week to fully activate your senses.

You can also post this on the Pinterest board 'Activating Your Senses' #senses

Questions or want more suggestions? Drop me a line.

Take action and share the love.

Forward to a friend and share what you felt with me via email, Facebook, LinkedIn, or Twitter. #senses

To your bliss!

GUIDE 6: YOUR INTUITIVE SELF

Are you curious when you hear people talking about 'trusting their gut', their intuition, or their higher self? Have you ever felt a connection to something bigger than you?

We make up to 35,0000 choices a day. Most of these choices are made intuitively, while a few are made consciously.

Our intuitive capacities make sense of our lives in far more complex ways than we are able to think logically. They are behind the scenes, making sense of energy, relationships, thoughts, feelings, physical space, memory, images and all of the sensory information that our body is picking up without us noticing.

If we do not walk or exercise, we lose muscle strength and soon we cannot walk. On the other hand, if we walk daily, our muscles get toned and strong. If we have not paid attention to our intuition, the signal is weak. Fortunately, we can strengthen our trust and sense of intuition with regular practice.

The communication line will become strong, it will stay open and grow and be there whenever you choose to connect. Like a guardian angel who is invisible. And when we choose to open up the communication channel, it is there.

It is similar to our relationships. We can have strong relationships and a deep connection with someone even though we may not see them very often, and when we do see them, the communication between us flows.

On the other hand, if our connection with someone is weak, we may not even remember them. When we do remember them, we can re-establish an intention to build the relationship and our connection becomes strong again. The same can be said for our intuition.

It is like forgetting a long-time friend is there, present for us, whenever we show up and ask them to relate to us. You may not even realise that there are signals that have been trying to get through to you.

When you start to pay attention, they get stronger. Now you start to feel something inside your body. For some it may be:

- A warm glow inside
- An expansion
- A tenderness
- A felt 'knowing'
- Or something else.

The way you sense and trust your intuition is unique to you.

Do not compare or judge the way you connect with your intuition with how others do. If you seek out a specific type of connection based on how someone else describes how they connect with their intuition, you may feel disappointed. Find your unique way by following the process that I suggest here, which will help you find your own unique methods.

You are unique and whatever opens up for you is perfect for you. Let go of imagining a connection that will look or feel a certain way. Be open to whatever emerges for you.

A guide to evoking your intuitive knowing

The following guide can evoke a connection through imagery and physical sensations of an intuitive knowing.

Read through my guide. Go to my website if you would like to purchase the exercises on audio.

Choose a time where you are comfortable and you have 10–15 minutes to yourself. Find a comfortable place, settle yourself and breathe. Imagine that I am guiding you on a journey to connect to your intuitive knowing.

I am not taking you where I want you to go. I am assisting you in finding your opening. You will go wherever the 'right' place is for you. Give your imagination its freedom to take you to a connection with your intuitive self, your higher self or, for some readers, to spiritual guidance or an angelic realm. Allow yourself to make a connection with another form of knowing beyond the rational.

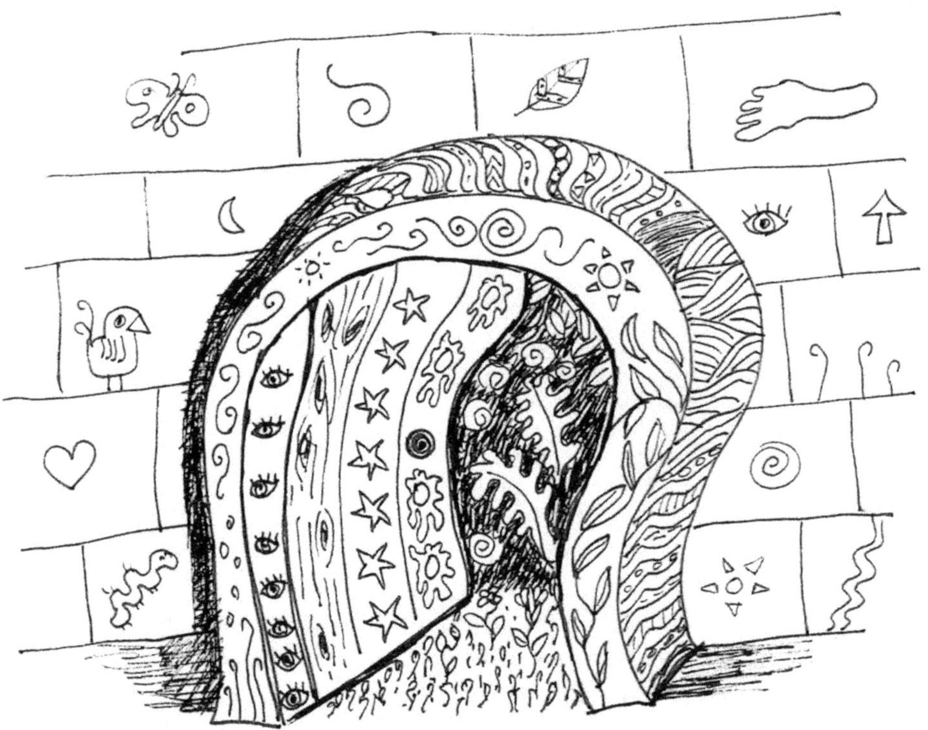

Be open and create an intention to invite your intuitive knowing to reconnect a lost link. Be relaxed. If you have your arms and legs crossed and you are uncomfortable, just wriggle around until you are comfortable. Open your arms so they are not crossed. Uncross your legs, be relaxed and open.

Take a breath in and a breath out. Breathe in again, and breathe out. Take another deep breath in, and one more breath out. Sigh or shake your body to relax. Take a moment to create a feeling of being at ease with me guiding you to sense grace and gratitude of the possibility of opening to your intuitive knowing.

Settle into your body.

Imagine you are on a journey, and on this journey you feel everything that there is to feel that is within you.

Imagine you are walking down a path feeling at ease, with grace and gratitude for all of who you are and your life—and this feeling amplifies with each step you take.

Look around. Imagine you are in a beautiful place. The kind of place that feels both safe and sacred to you. Feel secure and loved. You could be walking in a park, a forest, up a mountain or along a beach. Perhaps you are floating in space or swimming in the sea. Wherever you are, turn up the dial and gain clarity about what you are seeing, thinking, feeling, touching, hearing, tasting.

What is the sky like? What is around you? Are there trees? Are there flowers or is it an open space with just hills or the sea? Check that you are in a place where you feel safe, blessed, and nourished.

Keep walking and listen for sounds. There could be birds. There could be the roar of the sea or a plane. Perhaps you are in the sea like a mermaid and can hear water gurgling or the waves lapping against a shoreline. Feel the temperature of the air. Are you warm? What colours are you seeing? Feel the warmth of the sun on your skin. Feel the wind, if there is any—through your hair and across your face. Smell any scents from the sea, mountain or country location. Is it the sea that you can smell? If there are flowers, can you smell the perfume?

As you amplify what you see, hear and smell, allow the energy of the location to wash over you as if it is nourishment. Look up and see a space that looks inviting to rest. Sit down and embrace this beautiful space. It is amazing, being in this sacred haven. Just be present to how welcoming it is. How loved do you feel? Be there for a moment.

Out of the corner of your eye, catch a glimpse of someone coming towards you. The first glimpse is only a movement walking towards you. You are unsure who is walking your way but you feel safe. As this being comes closer, there is clarity about who your guardian is and what they look like. Your guardian, who represents your intuition, can come in any form. It could be an animal spirit. It could be from the sea. It could be someone that you've loved who may have passed away. It could be somebody who you don't know at all. This being is coming towards you. As it comes closer and closer, you're starting to see more and more clearly.

The closer they come the more you feel the presence of love and connectedness in your being. This guardian is here for your highest good. Your guardian wants you to know that whenever you want his or her presence, you can invite them to talk to you. The more you make an invitation, the more you will see, feel, hear, and sense the wisdom from your guardian. Your guardian may have a name. The more you feel a strong presence, the more you will be able to interpret intuitive messages. The messages may come through a sensory feeling in your gut. If so, it may help you to walk to pick up the sense in your gut. The deeper your connection, the more you will feel the sense whenever you choose. It may take a while to experiment with what your gut messages are saying. Experiment first with sensing a strong 'yes', 'no', or 'maybe' to a question.

Sometimes a message may surface as an image. Experiment with drawing with your non-dominant hand. Draw anything that comes to mind. Let your hand flow. Invite the drawing to speak to you. Sometimes you may sense a message as a feeling, or once again, perhaps someone comes into your life and says just the right word that opens a new awareness. You'll think, "Oh, wow." That is synchronicity, that is intuition, and it will be your intuition sensing messages of awareness in different forms.

If an image of your intuition or a guardian has emerged, take a moment to infuse the presence of this image into your memory.

Take a little bit of time being with whatever is there, like getting to know a new friend. Ask a question and give yourself the space and time to see if a message emerges. Give up controlling or forcing an outcome. Sometimes the simplest things that emerge generate a profound insight and a shift in our awareness and sense of being.

When you're ready, I would like you to think about what has been communicated to you. Give gratitude for what has emerged in any form. Know that the more you invite your intuition to connect, the more the connection becomes clearer and stronger. Send an invitation to your intuition to communicate in ways that the messages become stronger.

Look around and remember the image of this safe, loving place. Know that you can return whenever you want. Know that you have a place within you that is safe, nourishing and loving. Drink it into your body, breathe and stand up in your imagination. Say goodbye, knowing how to return. Walk back through the path, through the forest, or hills, or along the beach, wherever you have been and return to the room where you are sitting.

Take a breath. Let it out. Take another breath, and let it out. When you're ready, let the experience end.

The above guided visualisation has as many different responses as there are people. This is a description of one person's response after the visualisation.

Julie (name changed)

"There were three different places I imagined I was in all at once. One was in the sea. Especially when you said mermaid. I went to the place that I have been painting recently. I also walked along a beach and followed a path into a little forest. I kept switching between these three places.

"I met a dolphin who spoke to me in the sea. At the beach, I was with my partner. In the forest, I had an image of an angel with curls in her hair. I resonated with the angel."

At times we share our imagination with our trusted friends and at times we learn to sense that some images and sensations are best kept private.

If different images surface, they may all have different messages and be present for different purposes.

Each image may be interpreted as a part of ourselves. Our different selves have unique messages for our well-being.

On completion of reading or listening to a visualisation, you may have a sense of needing to complete the process by:

- Drawing the images you imagined or allowing yourself to draw freely
- Listening to music
- Moving, walking or dancing
- Collecting a sacred object that reminds you of this experience and creating an altar table
- Going into nature and walking, sensing your intuition as a guide walking by your side.

ENDINGS AND NEW BEGINNINGS

A new beginning is to end and come back to the place where you are at, but know it better and differently and receive a richer experience.

There is no greater agony than bearing an untold
story inside you. I've learnt that people will
forget what you said, people will forget what you
did, but people will never forget how you made
them feel. I know why the caged bird sings.
—Maya Angelou

An Invitation

Create a #trustyoursenses quest. Share what you have learnt on facebook, twitter, instagram Write to me and share your stories of what embodied wisdom you are uncovering.

#trustyoursenses quest

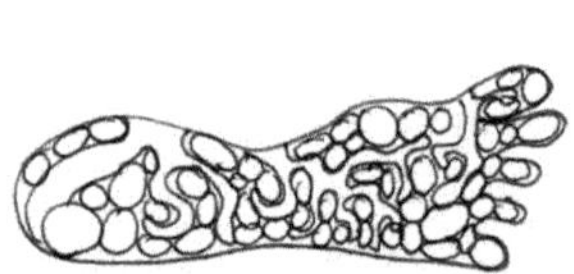

Keep a journal and draw. Write notes to build up rich body information as a body wisdom explorer.

Share your insights to help others. This is evolutionary knowledge that you are developing.

Share with me on:

twitter use the hash tag #senses https://twitter.com/deborahlange

facebook https://www.facebook.com/deblangepage

linked in http://au.linkedin.com/in/deborahlange

Working with Deb

Deb Lange is an Author, Advisor and Master of The Fine Art of Facilitation. She has over 35 years experience working in, advocating for and learning how to engage through embodied experience.

From corporate corridors to the red earth of the outback, buddhist monastery's to African fire ceremonies, Deb has learned from and lead with some of the world's most innovative minds.

Deb has an M.Ap.Sc (Hons) in Social Ecology, Degrees in Business and Education, Certificates in Social Artistry, Equine Facilitation, Interplay and much more. She designs for the whole person, body, mind and energy practices and philosophy in her experiential work. Deborah enables people to improvise with voice, movement and story to experiment, express, connect and play together as we sense our way into wisdom.

Do you want to deepen these skills?

Subscribe to my museletter at www.deblange.com for additional resources on how you can sense your way to wisdom. www.deblange.com.

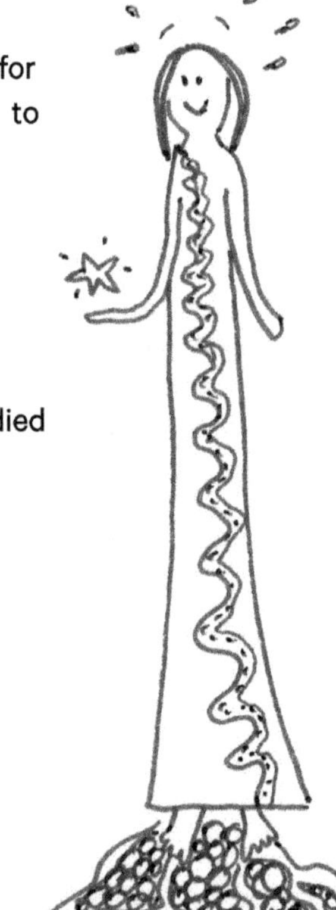

Videos and Audios ecourse

Want to practise some more? I have created an ecourse of 36 videos and audios to listen in, practise exercises and support you to discover how to learn from your embodied wisdom. www.deblangecourses.com.

Have questions about a Mentoring program?

Drop me a line at deb@deblange.com.au

Want more?

Invite me to speak, design and host an experiential workshop, conference or event in your community or organisation.

I work in-house or publicly anywhere in the world.

Email at deb@deblange.com.au

Please maintain the integrity of the work by acknowledging the source.

About the Illustrator

My heartfelt appreciation goes to Dr Sue Stack who resonated so closely with my work and drew the beautiful images to inspire and connect readers to their own. Sue reserves copyright over all the illustrations.

http://www.stack.bigpondhosting.com/

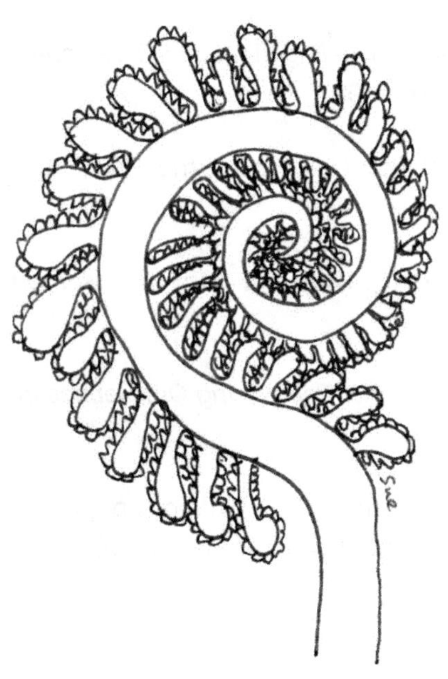

Reading List

David Abram, *Becoming Animal: An Earthly Cosmology*, 2011

Wade Davis, *The Wayfinders: Why Ancient Wisdom Matters in the Modern World*, 2009

Victor E Frankl, *Man's Search For Meaning: The classic tribute to hope from the Holocaust*, 2011

Howard Gardner, *Frames of Mind, The Theory of Multiple Intelligences*, 2011

William Glasser, *Choice Theory, A New Psychology of Personal Freedom*, 1999

Thich Nat Hahn, *Peace Is Every Step: The Path of Mindfulness in Everyday Life*, Bantam Books, 1991

Dr Jean Houston, *The Possible Human; A Course in Enhancing Your Physical, Mental, and Creative Abilities*, 1997

Daniel Kahneman, *Thinking Fast and Thinking Slow*, Farrax Strous Griroux, New York, 2011

Richard Kearney, *Anatheism: Returning to God after God*, 2011

Peter Levine, *Waking the Tiger: Healing Trauma: The Innate Capacity to Transform Overwhelming Experiences*, Levine, 1997

Dr. Bruce Lipton, *Biology of Belief: Unleashing the Power of Consciousness, Matter & Miracles*, 2015

Phil Porter & Cynthia Winton-Henry, *What the Body Wants, From the Secrets of Interplay*, 2004

Phillip Shepherd, *New Self, New World: Recovering Our Senses in the Twenty-First Century*, 2011

Rudolph Steiner, *Rudolf Steiner in the Waldorf School: Lectures and Addresses to Children, Parents, and Teachers* (Foundations of Waldorf Education)

Testimonials

"For as long as I've known Deb Lange she has aspired to bring all of herself — body, mind and spirit — to everything she has done. She has, in addition, learned how to help others to do the same. With her assistance, people learn to tune in to their instincts.

In applying this learning Deb has designed and facilitated engaging activities: activities that involved participants wholly. At such work, I regard her as one of the most skilled practitioners I know. In addition I have found her a person of decency and integrity. This shows through in the work she does.

Now, she has captured her wisdom and experience in this book. She has made her wisdom and experience available to the rest of us in the form of practical activities. This is a timely gift, I believe, very relevant to the world we currently inhabit. And even more relevant to the future world I think we face."

Bob Dick, Independent Scholar and Retired Professor

"Deb brings new insights into how to tune into our physicality, like learning a new inner language that is there to guide us. When we lean in to our senses and find our inner authority we develop a renewed appreciation of ourselves and our "joie de livre". This in turn affects the appreciation we have with one another and beauty in life. I recommend this book to anyone searching for answers, as this book, does not tell you the answers but, rather helps you discover your answers for yourself."

Miha Pognacik, Global Visionary, Speaker and Violinist

"Dear Deb,

Your book is a gem and is of such high quality such that it turns into a difficult issue for me to write a testimonial reaching the level you attained in writing this book. Still, I shall try.

Upon reading this book my mind and senses moved in many flows. Each flow unfolded many new ideas for me. Like a fern plant requires elements to grow, so too for a human being to go with the flow needs the right conditions. Ideas need moisture to dampen them, nutrients to feed them, right conditions to unfold their buds and reproduce. Ideas also flow and connect with another idea, mate with it and reproduce. We humans too need to grow and reproduce and we can only do that if we don't disintegrate ourselves into parts and make parts more important than the whole. We are fractal beings and our approaches should be based on this concept. If we want to grow and survive we need to keep our integrity and know use reductionist approaches for specific purposes.

This is what this book does. The beauty of this book is its integrity with our whole self, body, mind and soul in relationship to others. Humans have brains to think, emotions to feel, senses that lead us to generate beliefs and values that lead to choices and actions. Some of our beliefs and actions do not necessarily serve us well. This book guides us to sense how our actions are in integrity or not with our beliefs and whether we need to change either our beliefs or our actions. Deborah guides us to think and to connect with our senses and our intuition to help us grow.

This book reminds us to look for actions that lead us towards negativity are often triggered by memories and residues of past unresolved experiences. When we sense somebody trying to control us we may react emotionally if this person reminds us of our controlling parents and how they reduced our choices and what our hearts desired.

Deborah has found a way out of being constrained by experiences from the past, and it works. It is by having an integral approach to guide us to drop the leaves of irritating past experiences, to grow and express who we really are and give our lives new meaning. This is where this book stands out.

It takes all human senses, intuition, feelings and logic into consideration to work together to identify the obstacles that slow us down, accepting them and then transcend those past limitations by acquiring new skills. The best theory is an applied theory and it is where this book excels. Deb Lange enriches the book with a bundle of real life examples showing a sequential procedure on how to synchronize our senses and logical thinking to arrive at solutions for difficult human and business issues. The beauty of her approach is that Deb works with nature and not against it. New science shows that even plants may have a thinking process and the plants know how to mesh their senses and memories with their thinking to advance and grow. As we search and feed our brains with information from our senses so many new facts and solutions unfold. The book explains vividly the why and how to do this in a simple; yet profound, natural and applicable approach.

To grow and unfold new realities is how the fern plant grows and survives. This book is the fern for us to grow in harmony with our environment and ourselves. Nature provides us with examples and Deborah Lange developed a likewise approach. This book is a must read."

Ali Anani, Phd, Managing Partner/ Phenomena Communications

"I had a great opportunity of being personally coached by Deb, and with her guidance, my life turned completely 180 degrees! From feeling small to feeling empowered, from not having a voice to knowing WHEN and HOW to speak up greatly improved my relationships - with myself, with my family, with my spouse and with my coworkers, to the point that I rose from being a tired, overworked employee to being hailed as the best in my company to now following my dreams of being a writer and speaker. By having this book in your hand, is like being coached by her! Be ready to have all the cells in your body and your life be transformed!"

Van Bradshaw, Author and Speaker

www.ingramcontent.com/pod-product-compliance
Lightning Source LLC
Chambersburg PA
CBHW062042090426
42740CB00016B/2986